THE COMPLETE BOOK OF
CATS

THE COMPLETE BOOK OF
CATS

JUDITH A STEEH

Bison Books Limited

This edition published 1982 by
Bison Books Limited
4 Cromwell Place, London SW7

ISBN 0 86124 083 9

Printed in Hong Kong

Contents

Below : Tabby Persian kittens

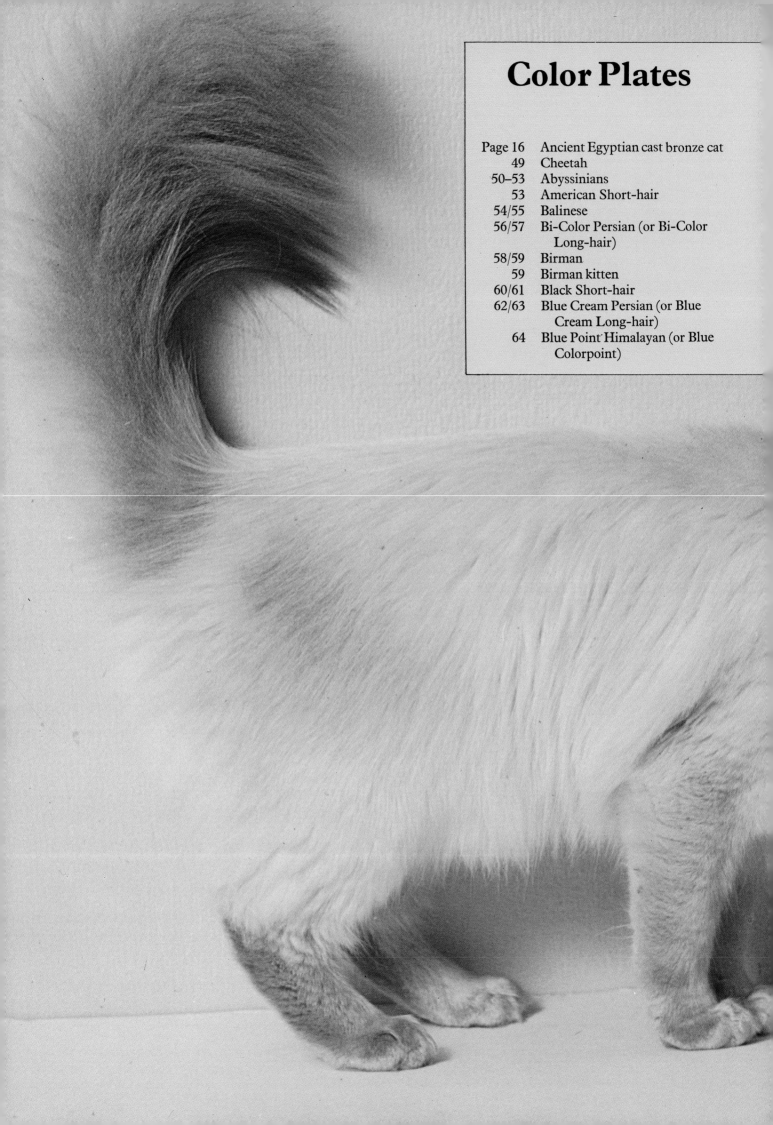

Color Plates

Below : Blue Point Balinese

Above : European Lynx

Introduction

Cats are extraordinary animals, and re-actions to them run the gamut from fear and loathing to adoration and worship.

Although few people are true ailuro-phobes, and even fewer would go to the same lengths as the ancient Egyptians, shaving their eyebrows and mourning for months over the death of a kitten, it is still worth considering how a small, relatively insignificant animal like the domestic cat can inspire such strong reactions. (Big cats, too, are often feared or revered, but in their case the reasons appear to be at least understandable.)

The most common reason given for dis-liking cats is their cool, independent, aloof attitude. They seem silent, predatory creatures, accepting sustenance and affec-tion from the misguided humans who keep them, and offering nothing in return. The fact is, of course, that cats *are* mysterious – and it is part of human nature to fear that which we do not understand.

But cat lovers, on the other hand, would point out that it is entirely possible to win a cat's affection and even devotion – and that if companionship with a cat is harder to achieve, that makes it even more valu-able. Cats communicate far less with their voices than do dogs, but anyone who takes the trouble to learn their 'body language' will soon discover that they are not nearly so inscrutable.

Left : Abyssinian mother and her kitten

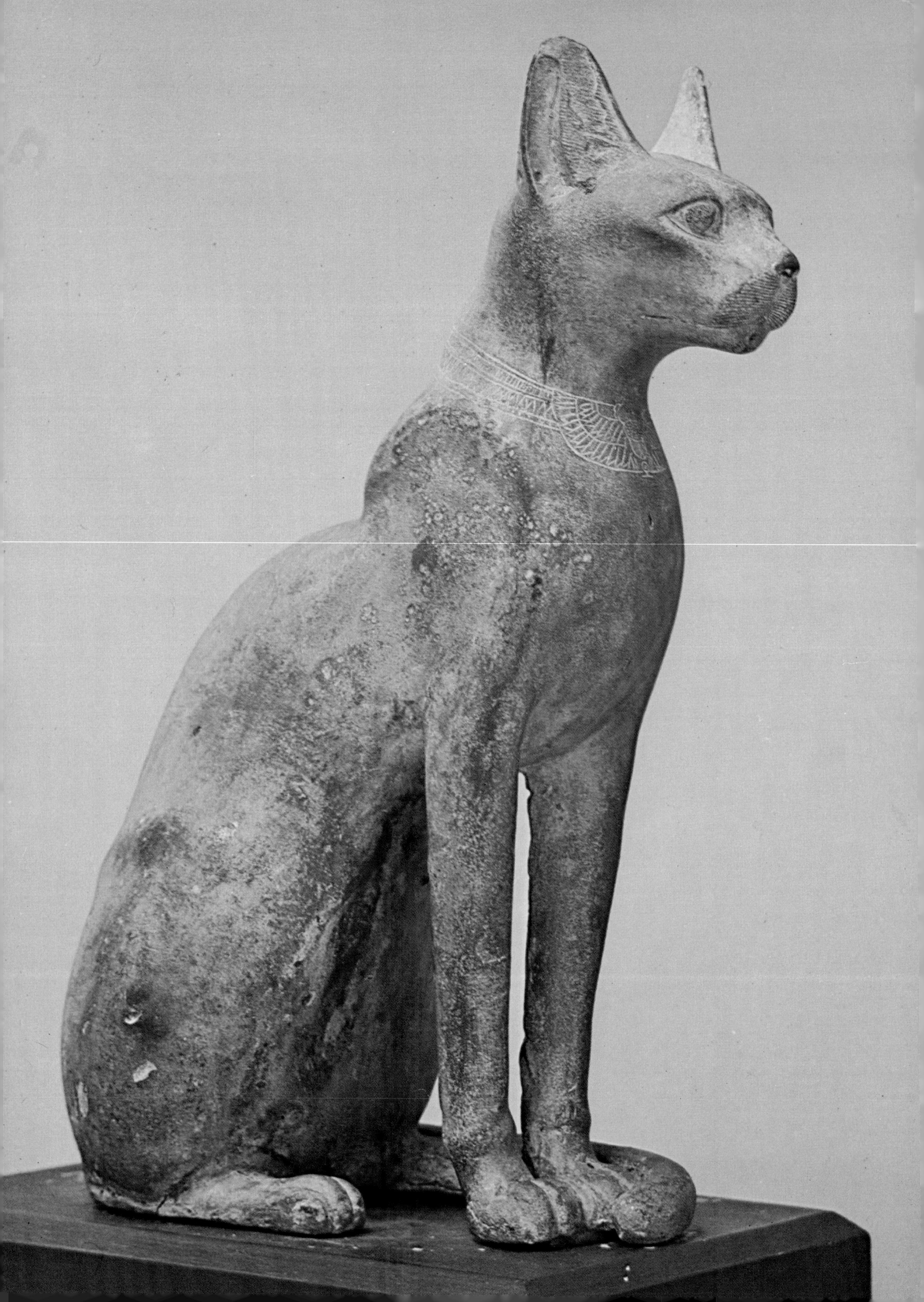

This ancient Egyptian Bronze figure was cast in the Saite Period about 600 BC. It resides now in the Cairo Museum.

Cats in History

Origins

Cats, or *Felidae*, are found throughout the world, but all – big or small, wild or domesticated – have so much in common that scientists have not formally subdivided them. This and other evidence strongly suggests that all cats had a common ancestor.

The first cats appeared in the Oligocene era, about 20 million years ago. There were two types: one, *Holophoneus*, produced *Smilodon*, the saber-tooth tiger and the other, *Dimictis*, eventually evolved into the modern day cat.

Dimictis was smaller than *Holophoneus*, faster, more agile, and much more intelligent. This, then was the ancestor of the almost 40 different cat species recognized today.

No one knows how or when domestic cats appeared on the scene. They are almost certainly mixtures of several species of wild cat (in scientific terms they are of *polyphyletic origin*). The earliest records state that domestic cats came from Egypt and are only about 5000 years old (dogs have been domesticated for at least 20,000 years). Short-haired cats were exported from Egypt to the European continent by the Phoenicians and to the New World by European colonists.

Ancient Egypt

The heyday of the domestic cat was certainly in ancient Egypt, where the pets were not only useful members of society, but for almost 2000 years were deified as well.

The fertile Nile Valley was the granary of the ancient world, and rats and mice must have caused severe damage before the cat appeared on the scene. In addition, cats were trained to hunt snakes, birds, and other small mammals, and even to retrieve ducks for hunters.

No one knows exactly why or when the Egyptian cat came to play such an important role in religion, but probably the reason for its deification was a complex mixture of respect for its hunting abilities, love of its beauty, and awe of its mysterious 'magical' personality. Paintings, sculptures, and tomb decorations portray a short-haired elegant cat very similar in size and shape to today's Abyssinian.

The cat goddess Bastet (or Bast or Pasht) was the daughter of Isis (goddess of the sun, moon, and earth) and Ra (god of the sun and the underworld). Worship of Bastet (and her representative, the cat) reached its peak around 950 BC. Beginning as the goddess of sexuality and fertility, she became the sun, moon, motherhood, and love goddess as well, in addition to protecting the dead, decreeing the success or failure of crops, making rain, and helping heal the sick, especially children.

More than 700,000 pilgrims traveled by boat to Bubastis each spring for her festival which was the gayest of the year. The appearance of the boats loaded with singing, dancing people was a signal to those who remained at home in cities along the way to begin their own festival.

Although there are several accurate accounts of the pilgrims' journey to Bubastis, no one seems to know exactly what went on when they got there. Some historians limit the attractions to good music, food, and wine while others describe the festival as a huge drunken sexual orgy. There were, at any rate, many parades, and the atmosphere was probably very like that at Mardi Gras or Oktoberfest.

Egyptian cats had either short ears and blunt noses or long ears and sharp noses. Most were short-haired and ginger-colored with black markings. They were spoiled and pampered by peasant and pharaoh alike; mummified cats have been found wearing necklaces, earrings, and even nose rings. When they died cats were given elaborate funerals, and the household where the death occurred was plunged into deepest mourning. Even poor families held a wake for their pet, and the bereaved owners shaved their eyebrows to demonstrate their grief.

For a long time it was illegal to harm a cat in Egypt, and the crime was punishable by death. Herodotus, who was usually quite accurate about things he saw firsthand (if a bit credulous when it came to believing other travelers' stories), gives a graphic description of an unfortunate Egyptian who happened to witness the death of a cat – trembling, bathed in tears, loudly proclaiming to all and sundry that he had had no part in the matter. Perhaps there was good reason for this extreme behavior – one Roman soldier was literally torn to pieces by an infuriated mob in Thebes after he accidentally killed a cat.

By about 100 BC cat worship was in decline and Phoenician traders, who had been trying for years to smuggle cats to a rodent-ridden world, were finally able to export them in quantity. The best days had come to an end.

Europe

Below : In contrast to the photograph on the preceding page is this picture of a living *Bronze Egyptian Mau. This breed and the Abyssinian share the dubious distinction that their ancestors were the cat deities of ancient Egypt.*
Inset : A short-haired white cat of Foreign or Oriental type. The Foreign type is said to have originated in Egypt.

By the end of the fifth century AD the domestic cat was well established in the Middle East and Europe. As the barbaric invasions brought rats and plague sweeping across the continent, cats rose in value. In several countries in fact (including Wales and Switzerland), there were laws governing the sale and protection of cats.

Unfortunately, during the Dark Ages the cat became an outcast. Cats never quite lost the supernatural, pagan reputation they had acquired in Egypt, and they were soon caught up in a wave of witch-hunting and persecutions. There are horror stories by the dozen of cats – hundreds of thousands of them – being burned, flayed, crucified, and thrown from the tops of towers, usually under the auspices of the Church.

Paradoxically, the cat was saved by the Black Death. Returning Crusaders brought with them the Asiatic black rat, carrier of the bubonic plague. With so few cats left the rats bred unhindered, and in only two years in the middle of the fourteenth century three out of every four people in Europe died of the disease. Those who had sometimes literally risked their lives to keep cats now came into their own; their homes and farms were relatively free from rats. Gradually the authorities saw the light and ended their persecution.

By the end of the Renaissance cats were again valued members of society. Cardinal Wolsey in England insisted on taking his cat with him to the cathedral and to royal conferences. In France Montaigne, Richelieu, and Mazarin all doted on their pets, and Moncrif wrote his charming *Histoire des Chats*, the first cat book as we know it.

The Victorian Age found the cat prized not only as a useful pet, but as a thing of beauty. Cats were fashionable; the first cat show was held at Crystal Palace in

London in 1871. In 1895 an American version was held at Madison Square Garden, and the success of these shows began a tradition that continues to this day.

The New World

Domestic cats probably arrived in the Americas with Columbus or shortly thereafter – there were certainly only wild cats in the New World before it was colonized by Europeans.

In the early part of the eighteenth century cats traveled with the Jesuits as they moved up the west coast of Mexico. There were cats on the *Mayflower*, and in the middle of the seventeenth century many more were imported to help defeat a horde of black rats who were battling the colonists for their grain supplies.

Cats traveled with the French voyageurs on the great Midwestern waterways, and pushed westward with the wagon trains. As the Indians discovered the cat's hunting abilities the animals became valuable trading items, and later western miners paid as much as fifty dollars for a good mouser.

The Orient

Domestic cats probably arrived in China early in the Han dynasty (206 BC–221 AD) and were soon firmly entrenched in Chinese society.

The first known litter of kittens in Japan was born on 19 September 999 in the Imperial Palace in Kyoto. It was the Emperor Ichijo's thirteenth birthday and he was so completely entranced by the small animals that he ordered the kittens to be given the same care that royal infants usually received.

For several centuries cats in Japan belonged exclusively to royalty. But around the fourteenth century the growing silk industry was threatened by mice. Cats, who were by then more numerous, became even more valuable and closely guarded. Finally the authorities were forced to decree that all cats were to be set loose, and that it was forbidden to buy or sell them.

Today cats are highly regarded in both China and Japan – in the former, more for their prowess in hunting rodents, and in the latter perhaps more for their beauty and charm.

Cats in Folklore and Myth

The larger members of the cat family appear in the myths and legends of almost every country in the world, and the domestic cat too, has a place in that tradition.

There were no domestic cats in Eden – only lions, tigers, panthers, and leopards – and in fact the Bible does not mention cats at all (perhaps because they were being worshiped as pagan gods in nearby Egypt at roughly the time the Bible was being written). But legend has it that during the long weeks afloat in the Ark the rat and mouse population increased so alarmingly that the rodents soon threatened the safety of the entire ship. Noah, rising to the occasion, passed his hand three times over the head of the lioness, and she obligingly sneezed forth a cat who soon dealt with the problem.

The ancient Greeks had another story of the cat's creation – one of the few times the animals are mentioned in their literature. Apollo, it seems, created the lion and sent it to frighten his sister Diana. The Huntress was not so easily intimidated however, and promptly created the domestic cat as a parody to poke fun at her brother's monster. Diana was also goddess of the moon, an association cats had held earlier in Egypt and retained for centuries thereafter.

According to an old Norse legend, Utgard-Loki, king of the giants, had a giant cat; and of course Freyya, goddess of love and marriage, rode in a chariot pulled by two cats.

Cats hold a special place in the Arab world, as Selema held a special place in Mohammed's heart. It is written that once in Damascus the prophet cut off his sleeve rather than disturb his sleeping cat when it was time for prayers. A Sultan in Cairo was the first man known to have left a legacy for stray cats. Cats figure in several tales in the *Arabian Nights*, and Burton claims that the word 'tabby' comes from a quarter of Baghdad called Attabi that is famous for its watered or streaked silks.

Every country has tales of cats that take human form or vice versa. In Japan, cats with long tails were said to have this power – which may either account for or be accounted for by the fact that the native cats of Japan have very short tails. In Japan too, black cats were considered good luck as they were thought able to cure disease especially in children, but red or

Above: Cream Persian.
Below: The lucky (or unlucky) but always mysterious black cat.

pink cats were thought to have supernatural powers and were avoided.

During the fourteenth century the black cat was well known as either a witch or a devil in disguise, and these poor creatures took the brunt of the feline persecutions during the Dark Ages.

Today, however, whether or not one avoids black cats depends on where one lives. In the United States and Ireland the old superstitions persist, and a black cat crossing one's path always means bad luck.

But in England and Scotland black cats bring good luck. English sailors purchased them for their wives, believing that as long as the cat was contented the weather would be fair, and in Scotland a black cat in the house ensured that the young ladies who lived there would have plenty of beaux.

Black cats are also considered good luck in the Orient. Chinese sailors carried them aboard ship to bring favorable winds.

Cats in the Arts

Cats in Literature

Cats and writers seem to have an affinity for each other, and the list of famous writers who owned, were fond of, and in many cases, wrote about cats would be long indeed. From Lord Byron to Mark Twain, from Henry James to Ernest Hemingway, Dickens, Wordsworth, Baudelaire – the names span the history of poetry and prose on every continent.

During medieval times animal stories were very popular, as they had always been – and still are today. Many of these stories were collected into *Bestiaries,* collections of descriptions of the habits of various animals, each followed by a 'signification' that derived a Christian moral from the story. One of the few fragments remaining of the Anglo-Saxon *Physiologus* is the story of the Panther, and the more complete Middle English *Beastiary* contains 'The Lion.'

The first text devoted entirely to the domestic cat appeared during the latter half of the sixteenth century. Chaucer mused on the cat's preference for mice over milk in *The Manciple's Tale.*

Cats pop in and out of literature for the next three centuries, gradually becoming more likeable as time goes on. Cervantes has Don Quixote accuse a group of cats of witchcraft – a reference to the horrors of the Middle Ages, as is the witches' invocation of Graymalkin in *Macbeth.* In John Gay's fable 'The Rat-Catcher and Cats' the two factions eventually arrive at a working agreement. There are three rather important cats in Dicken's *Bleak House* (1852), belonging to Krook, Mr Jellyby and Mr Vohles. And who could forget Dinah in *Alice in Wonderland* or the Cheshire Cat in *Through the Looking Glass*?

Cats play starring roles in many more modern works by famous writers. Even the briefest list would have to include Kipling's *The Cat That Walked By Himself*; Poe's masterpiece of horror, *The Black Cat*; Hemingway's short story, *Cat in the Rain*; *The Cat* by Collette; and *The Malediction* by Tennessee Williams; not to mention *archy and mehitabel* by don marquis; and a number of excellent books by Paul Gallico.

Poets have been no less inspired by their pets: Thomas Gray wrote *Ode* in 1742; Horace Walpole's unfortunate cat Selima drowned in a tub of goldfish; Edward Lear

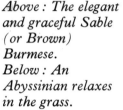

Above : The elegant and graceful Sable (or Brown) Burmese.
Below : An Abyssinian relaxes in the grass.

22

Above and Below: This sublime Abyssinian looks as if it could adorn the walls of an ancient tomb.

immortalized the marriage of *The Owl and the Pussycat*. Wordsworth, Blake (The Tyger), Yeats, Swinburne, and Hardy are just a few of the many others whose cats moved them to poetry.

The poetry of T S Eliot is justly famous for its erudition and social consciousness, but not often for its humor. In *Old Possum's Book of Practical Cats*, however, he reveals an entirely new side of his character in a witty, but always thoroughly sympathetic and knowledgeable series of poems about cats.

The poems address two very important topics, *The Naming of Cats* ('. . . a difficult matter, (that) isn't just one of your holiday games') and *The Ad-dressing of Cats*.

We are then introduced to a number of cats, all of whom are immediately recognizable. There is the Gumbie Cat, the tabby 'on whom well-ordered households depend . . .' and the Rum Tum Tugger, a perverse animal who '. . . will do as he do do and there's no doing anything about it!' The rather small, black and white Jellicle Cats rest up all day so that they can dance all night; the Great Rumpus Cat single-handedly routs a whole army of Pekes and Pollicles; Mr Mistoffelees, the original Conjuring Cat, not only spirits away various household items, but magically produces seven kittens. Maccivity, the

'Napoleon of Crime' baffles Scotland Yard while Gus the theater cat reminisces about his past triumphs on the boards. Bustopher Jones saunters toward one or another of his clubs in St James's and Skimbleshanks rides the Midnight Mail. And last, but never least, is Growltiger, a bargee known as 'The Terror of the Thames' who is finally forced to walk the plank by a gang of dastardly Siamese.

Furthermore, one of the best examples of indirectly using cat images to establish a mood is a stanza in T S Eliot's *The Love Song of J Alfred Prufrock*.

The study of cat literature *per se* can be a time-consuming but rewarding occupation. Anyone seriously interested in pursuing the topic would be well advised to consult Claire Necker's *Four Centuries of Cat Books, 1570–1970*, published by Scarecrow Press in 1972 – an annotated bibliography of cat books published in English.

The range in cat literature is enormous. There are adventurous cats like Dick Whittington's friend or Puss in Boots, and there are long-suffering cats as in Susannah Patteson's *Pussy Meow*. There are musical cats (*The King of Cats* by Stephen Vincent Benet), talking cats (*Tobermory* by Saki) and even cats who are FBI agents (*Undercover Cat* by The Gordons).

The largest number of cat books are written for children; the next largest sub-division covers cat care. There are also many general cat books (of which Agnes Repplier's *The Fireside Sphynx*, first published in 1901, is an excellent example), fiction, anthologies, picture books, cartoon books, and scientific books – anything in short, that strikes a reader's fancy.

Cats in Art

People have been drawing, painting, and sculpturing cats since the time of the ancient Egyptians. Often they were symbols of freedom and independence; cats appeared on the shields of Roman soldiers, on the coat of arms of the Dukes of Burgundy, and as symbols of freedom both in Holland during the Dutch struggle for independence in the sixteenth century, and again during the French Revolution.

During the thirteenth century the example of St Francis of Assisi led to many sympathetic portrayals of cats especially by Italian painters. Around 1450, the philosopher St Jerome was depicted with a feline companion by Antonello da Messino. But just as often cats represented evil. Ghirlandaio, Luini, and Cellini all painted Judas accompanied by a cat; St Ives, the patron saint of lawyers, was often shown with a cat said to represent all the evil qualities associated with that profession. In Dürer's engraving *Adam and Eve* (1504) the cat is a cruel symbol. Da Vinci's study of the cat however, reveals a scientific exploration of the cat's form.

In 1523 Guilio Romano would paint a threatening evil cat in *Madonna della Gatta*, but by the end of the century Federico Barocci was showing cats in a much more naturalistic manner – in, for example, *Holy Cat With Family* (1574) and *Annunciation* (1584). Cats were residents of the Garden of Eden in Breughel the Elder's *Paradise* in the early 1600s.

From that point on, the treatment of cats in western painting became increasingly sympathetic and naturalistic. Some of the most charming portrayals of cats include Jan Steen's *The Cat's Reading Lesson* (1650), Jean Baptiste Greuze's *The Wool Winder* (1759), Renoir's *Woman With A Cat* (1880) and Mary Cassatt's *Children Playing With a Cat* (1908).

Several artists in both east and west have achieved a certain measure of popularity by drawing or painting cats.

Gottfried Mind, a Swiss artist, became known as the 'Cat Raphael' in Europe at the beginning of the nineteenth century for his drawings and water colors that are almost photographic reproductions of the animals he loved.

During the mid-1800s, a Japanese artist named Kuniyoshi produced many portraits of cats that show both understanding and humor. His cats range from anthropomorphic representations (*The Cat Family at Home*, c.1840) to demons (*The Cat Witch of Okabe*), to realistic studies (*Cats for the Fifty-Three Stations of Tokaido Road*, 1848).

In England at the end of the century Louis Wain was an enormously popular illustrator whose drawings of cats appeared in countless children's books, magazines, and newspapers on both sides of the Atlantic. Unfortunately he went mad and was committed to an asylum in 1924. His popularity continued, but gradually his style changed until his drawings became more concerned with patterns than with accurate representations of cats. Today he is remembered by many for the way in which he helped popularize cats, and is also famous in psychiatry for the manner in which his growing schizophrenia expressed itself in his art.

Cats in Music

Cats have appeared in western music for many centuries. Songs about cats abound – children's songs, famous cat poems that have been set to music, and others like that most popular cat song of all, 'The Cat Came Back.'

Many instrumental pieces have been inspired by cats. Scarlatti and Liszt both composed pieces titled *The Cat's Fugue*, while Chopin produced the *Cat Valse*. Stravinsky wrote *Lullabies for the Cat*. Prokofiev used sensuous woodwinds to denote the cat in *Peter and the Wolf*, while Zey Confrey imitated a cat running over the piano in his jazz classic, *Kitten on the Keys*.

Tschaikovsky's famous ballet *The Sleeping Beauty* contains a famous scene in which two dancers, Puss in Boots and White Cat, imitate feline movements; there are many other dances inspired by cats, and ballet has even named one of its most difficult steps – the *pas de chat* – after them.

No one knows how much cats like human music, but some have certainly been active in the music world. Jenny Lind, for example, used to sing to her pet cat. Saint Saens was a noted cat lover, and Albert Schweitzer was seldom seen without a feline companion.

Cats Today

In many ways many cats lead better lives today than ever before. As the human standard of living rises, so does that of those pets lucky enough to have secured a seat on the gravy train. In America or Europe today, a domestic cat who has a home is likely to have a very comfortable one. The usefulness of cats in advertising and the enormous number of books about them published each year mirror the important place they hold in society's affections. The ever-increasing number of pet boutiques, specialist shops and cemeteries, also indicates their growing status in the eyes of their owners.

Unfortunately this happy picture only applies to a very few of the world's cats. In America alone more than 50 million kittens are born each year – but only a very small number live more than a few months. Millions die of cold, hunger, disease, or injuries. Millions more are put down in one of the nation's 2000 public shelters or pounds, simply because there are no facilities to keep them for more than 48 or 72 hours. Some will even be sold to laboratories in a desperate attempt to raise money to provide shelter to others. The fate of the kittens who are born strays is hard enough to contemplate. The thought of those callously abandoned in rubbish cans or on the roadside by their owners – who thought it cruel or found it inconvenient to have their pets neutered – is horrible.

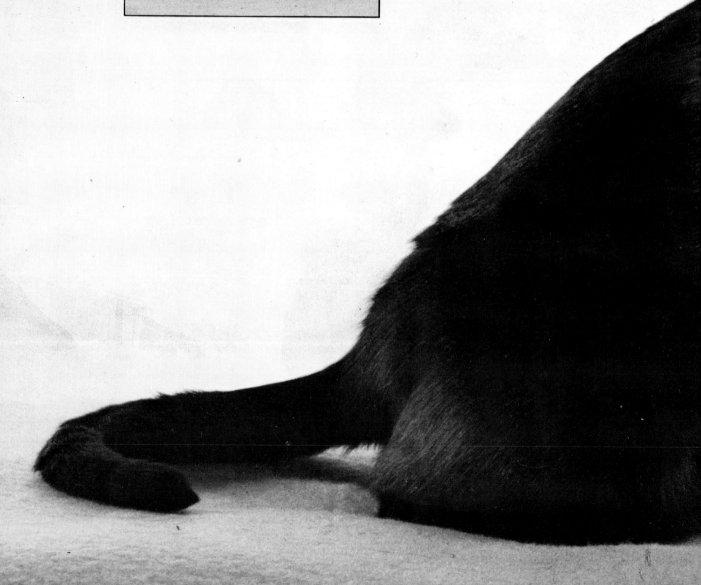

Wild cats find themselves in an equally unhappy though opposite situation. There is scarcely an entry for a wild cat in Section 3 (the Catalog Section) of this book that does not note that the species is in grave danger of extinction – either from intensive hunting, or from more impersonal threats such as the destruction of the animals' habitat through war or the encroachment of civilization. Zoos labor manfully to prevent the total extinction of many rare breeds, but all too often the end result is that the number of animals of a given species becomes restricted to but a few kept in captivity.

Cat lovers, then, have two battles to fight: overpopulation on the domestic front and declining population in the wild. Neither will be won easily, or quickly, or cheaply.

Left inset: Turkish Van Cat.
Above: A young White Short-hair.
Left: The Seal Point Siamese is perhaps the most popular pedigree house cat in the world today.

26

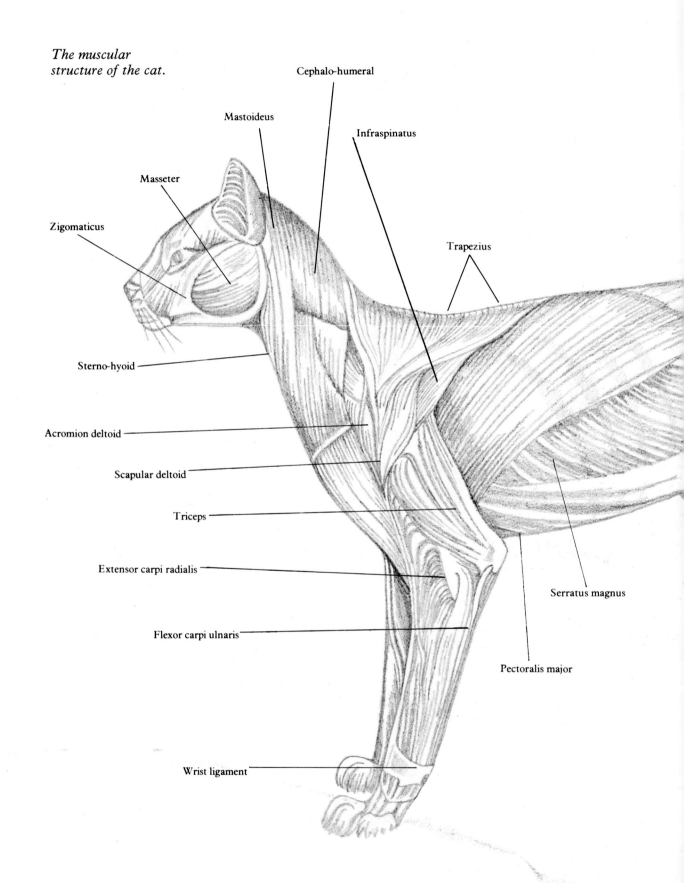

The muscular structure of the cat.

Cephalo-humeral

Mastoideus

Infraspinatus

Masseter

Zigomaticus

Trapezius

Sterno-hyoid

Acromion deltoid

Scapular deltoid

Triceps

Extensor carpi radialis

Serratus magnus

Flexor carpi ulnaris

Pectoralis major

Wrist ligament

Anatomy

Some knowledge of how cats' bodies are constructed and how they work is vital for every cat owner. Not only will it help an owner to understand his cat better, but it will be useful in daily care and will be of great value if the cat becomes ill.

Cats are mammals and thus share many common anatomical features with the other higher animals including man. All mammals have a backbone, mammary glands, a four-chambered heart, a muscular diaphragm, and vital organs such as lungs, spleen, liver, intestines, etc. Cats have hair – a feature scientists believe has helped many mammals adapt to drastic changes in climate – and bear their young alive. The fact that the babies depend on their mother for a relatively long time may be another reason the species has survived so well; the young have time to learn how to cope with a hostile world instead of relying solely on instinct to survive.

There are many other similarities between cat and human bodies. For example, only the cat's hind legs have knee joints. The front legs are jointed like elbows, and are attached to the shoulder bone like human arms.

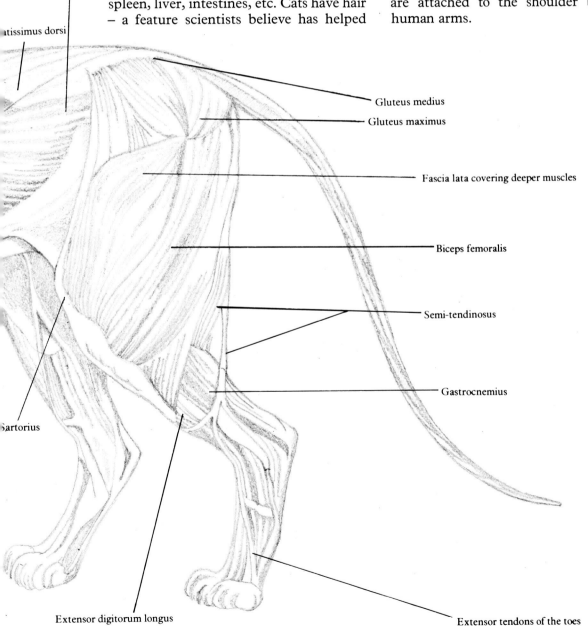

Great oblique

atissimus dorsi

Gluteus medius

Gluteus maximus

Fascia lata covering deeper muscles

Biceps femoralis

Semi-tendinosus

Gastrocnemius

Sartorius

Extensor digitorum longus

Extensor tendons of the toes

Skeleton

The purpose of the skeletal system is to support the body, to protect the soft inner tissues and organs, and to provide levers for moving body parts. As mentioned earlier, there are many similarities between cat and human skeletons, but there are several important differences too. Cats, for example, do not have opposable thumbs nor do they have collar bones. They have thirteen ribs compared to man's twelve, and tailbones.

Cats have from 230 to 290 bones; as with humans, younger animals have more separate bones, some of which fuse together with age.

The cat's skeleton is a strong framework that is flexible enough to provide great freedom of movement. Ball and socket

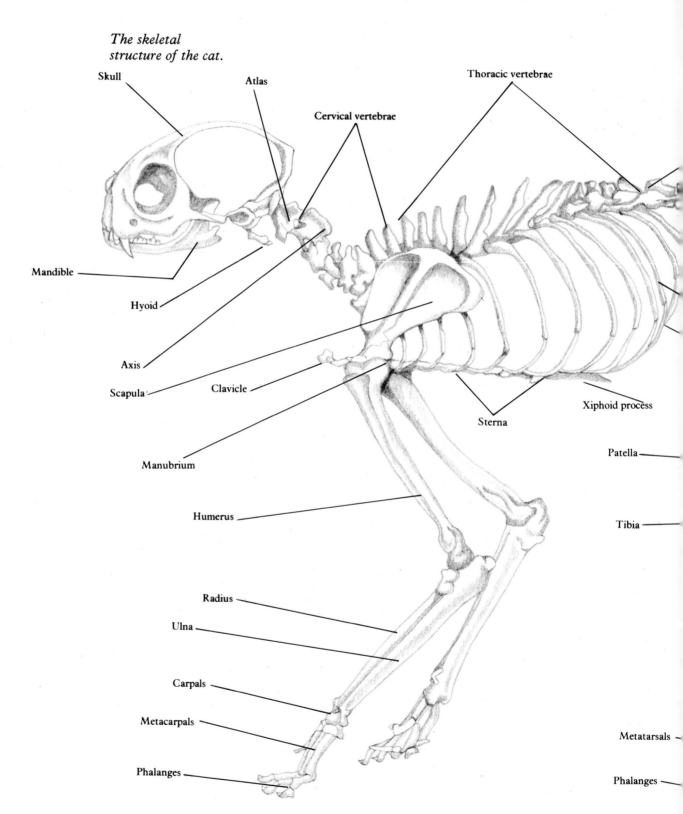

The skeletal structure of the cat.

Skull

Atlas

Cervical vertebrae

Thoracic vertebrae

Mandible

Hyoid

Axis

Scapula

Clavicle

Manubrium

Sterna

Xiphoid process

Patella

Tibia

Humerus

Radius

Ulna

Carpals

Metacarpals

Metatarsals

Phalanges

Phalanges

joints, like the hip joint, permit a wide range of movement and give the cat its agility in jumping and climbing. Hinge joints (for example, at elbow, knee, and jaw) and pivot joints (like the neck) which allow side-to-side movement are also useful.

The tail is an extension of the spinal cord and consists of 21–22 bones if the cat has a full tail. It is used primarily for balance in climbing and jumping. Many experts believe that the cat also uses it to help right itself when falling, by whipping it around to help turn the body in air. In addition, it is useful for communicating either pleasure (held stiff and straight) or anger (lashing from side to side or thrashing up and down).

The cat's smooth, gliding walk comes from the fact that unlike most other four-legged animals, it moves both right and both left feet forward at the same time.

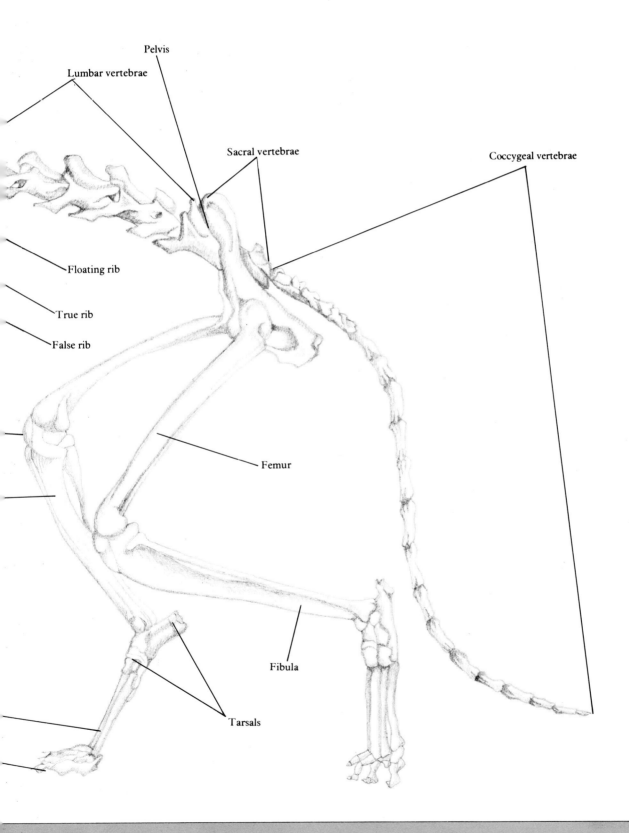

Pelvis

Lumbar vertebrae

Sacral vertebrae

Coccygeal vertebrae

Floating rib

True rib

False rib

Femur

Fibula

Tarsals

Hair and Skin

Cat hair acts as insulation by trapping a layer of air next to the body. By growing more hair in cold weather or by shedding it in warmer seasons, the amount of insulation can be partially controlled. It also protects the cat from insect bites, thorns, and many disease organisms. Thus the hair must be kept in good condition.

When a cat is frightened its hair stands upright. This is a protective mechanism to make the animal look larger and fiercer, and to frighten the attacker.

The cat's skin is a tough, flexible, waterproof membrane made up of two layers: the *epidermis* (outer layer) and *dermis* (inner layer). It contains sweat glands that help regulate body temperature; the cat's body is cooled by radiating heat, however, while human sweat glands cause inner cooling. The skin also has glands that secrete *sebum*, the oily substance that coats the hairs to protect them.

The pads on each of the cat's feet are composed of thick layers of specialized skin that can take a lot of punishment. There is a pad under the bones of each foot and one for each toe (*digit*); the front feet also have pads under the wrist bones. The foot pads contain sweat glands that discharge fluids to the outside.

Claws are also made of special skin cells, like human finger- and toenails. In all cats but the cheetah they can be retracted into folds above the digital pads when the cat is not using them to fight, climb, or hunt.

Below : Cat's paw showing the dew claw and carpal pad.

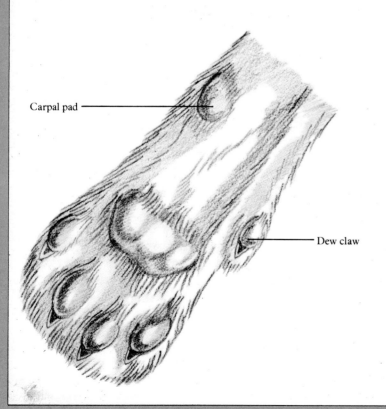

Carpal pad

Dew claw

Senses

Eyes

Cats' eyes, which have long fascinated people because of their shape and ability to see in the dark, are in fact very similar to human eyes.

The eyes are large, round globes protected by the skull; their movement is controlled by six different muscles. In the center of the eye a tiny hole, the *pupil*, expands or contracts (in most cats, to a linear slit) to allow the proper amount of light to enter. The pupil is surrounded by the colored part of the eye called the *iris*.

Behind the pupil, the *lens* bends the light rays so that they fall on the *retina*; the nerve cells in the retina send impressions to the brain via the *optic nerve*. Cats apparently cannot see colors (in fact, only birds and the higher primates have a color sense); a cat sees the world in shades of gray, like a black-and-white television image.

A special layer of cells on the retina, called the *tepetum*, acts as a mirror to collect all the available light and reflect it back into the eye. This helps account for the cat's exceptional eyesight, especially in the dark or even in regions like the ultraviolet. The tepetum is what makes cats' eyes shine in the dark.

The eyes have a transparent covering (the *cornea*) around which is a ring of white tissue called the *sclera*.

There is a third eyelid (the *nictating membrane*) in the lower part of the cat's eye for further protection. It is either pale pink or very dark, and can sometimes be seen when the animal is frightened or ill; veterinarians find it valuable for detecting some diseases or parasites.

Ears

Cats' ears, like human ears, contain mechanisms for both hearing and balance.

Most adult humans hear sounds that vibrate at around 20,000 cycles/second; mice hear at the rate of 100,000 cycles/second. A cat hears somewhere between 30,000 and 100,000 cycles/second – which is why most cats will respond better to higher-pitched voices, and can hear many sounds that are too faint or high-pitched for humans.

The outer ears are cupped, and the cat can aim them at a source to conduct the sound. Inside the eardrum three small

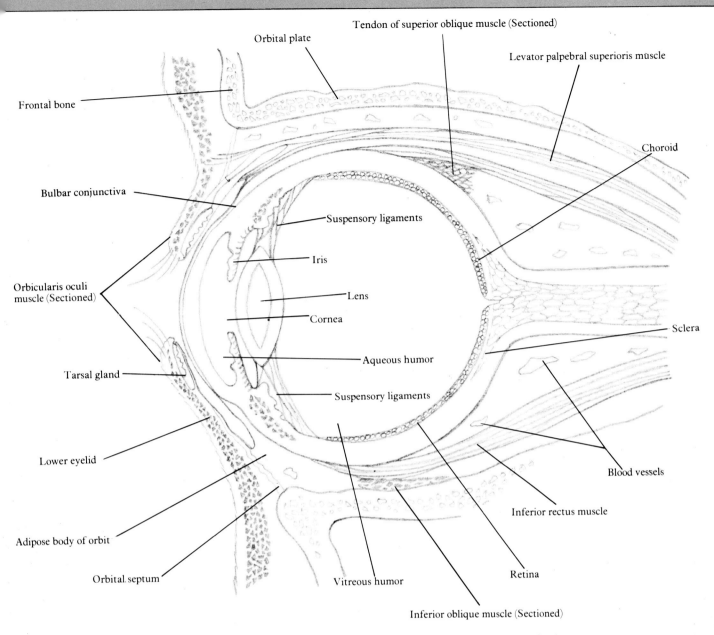

Frontal bone

Orbital plate

Tendon of superior oblique muscle (Sectioned)

Levator palpebral superioris muscle

Choroid

Bulbar conjunctiva

Suspensory ligaments

Iris

Orbicularis oculi muscle (Sectioned)

Lens

Cornea

Sclera

Aqueous humor

Tarsal gland

Suspensory ligaments

Lower eyelid

Blood vessels

Adipose body of orbit

Inferior rectus muscle

Orbital septum

Vitreous humor

Retina

Inferior oblique muscle (Sectioned)

bones (the *hammer*, the *anvil*, and the *stirrup*) transmit sounds into the *cochlea*, which contains the *auditory nerve*.

Nearby, the three horseshoe-shaped *semicircular canals* help the cat keep its balance. The canals are lined with nerve cells and filled with fluid. As the head moves, the fluid flows over the nerve endings with varying pressure which the brain is able to translate.

Nose

The cat's nose is small and can be any color or colors from pale pink to black. It is made up of several very tough layers of skin.

Cats have a more sensitive sense of smell than humans, but do not smell as well as dogs. Instead cats tend to rely more on sight and touch when hunting. They tend to dislike most of the same smells that humans do.

Above : The structure of a cat's eye. Cat's eyes have always been fascinating to mankind – not without reason.

Tongue

The most important tasting mechanism is the tongue which has taste buds that operate much like those in man. Like humans, cats have distinct and often idiosyncratic preferences and dislikes for certain tastes.

Whiskers

Whiskers grow on the cat's cheeks, above the eyes, and on the lip, extending out to about the width of the shoulders. When the tips of the whiskers brush an object they stimulate a nerve at the base of the hair, thus helping guide the animal through tall grass, shrubs, or perhaps even through dark rooms or tunnels.

Nervous System

The cat's nervous system is much like that of the dog, but it is more intricate, and the cat is usually more nervous and highly strung.

There are two basic parts to the nervous system: the central system (brain and spinal cord) and the peripheral system (sensory fibers gathered together in bundles called nerves). The cat's brain, like man's, is divided into the *cerebrum*, which controls conscious actions, and the *cerebellum*, which controls reflex and motor activities.

A cat's skull.

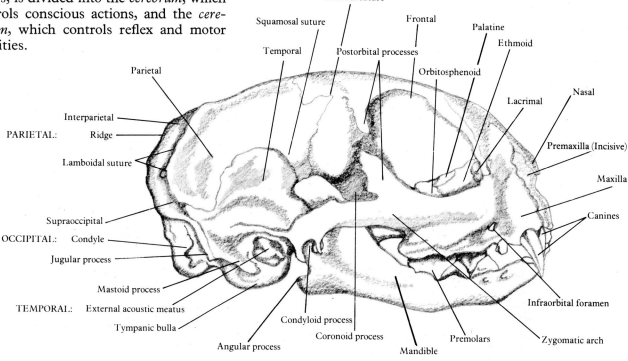

A cross-section of the vertebral column.

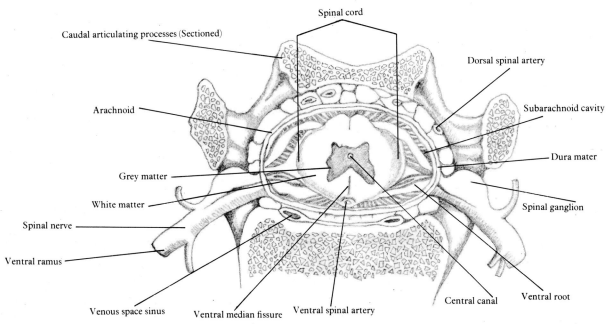

Respiratory System

Like other mammals, cats have a lung on each side of the chest separated by a partition. This separating membrane is very thin, and is easily damaged if the animal sustains a chest injury. If one of the cat's lungs collapses, the other will also.

Respiratory organs of the head.

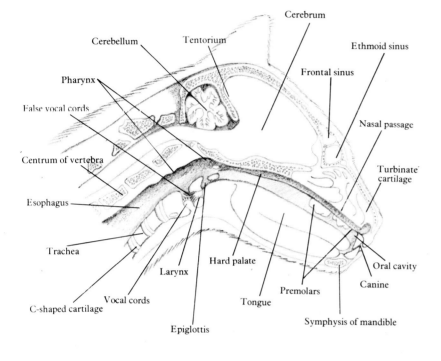

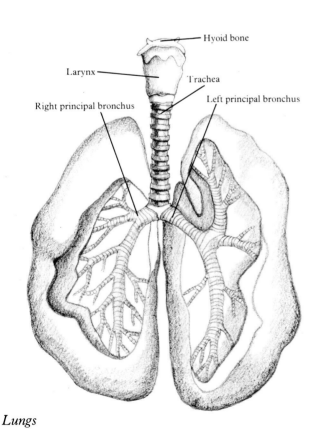

Lungs

Circulatory System

Cats are warm-blooded and have complex, highly developed circulatory systems.

Heart

The heart is located very near the lungs. It has four chambers, forming two pumps; one side circulates blood in the lungs and the other takes care of circulation in the rest of the body.

Blood

Cat's blood contains *red blood cells* to carry oxygen, *white corpuscles* to fight disease, and *platelets* which help the blood clot, all suspended in a fluid called *plasma*.

Spleen

The spleen is three to four inches long and is located behind the stomach. It acts as a filter and also stores blood.

Lymph Nodes

Lymph nodes are also filters, destroying bacteria and viruses in the blood.

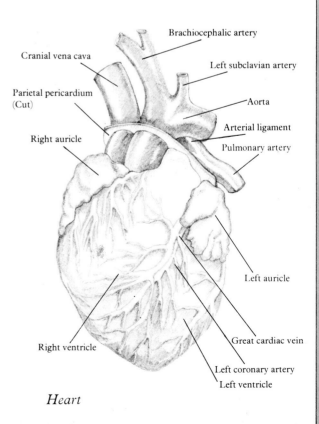

Heart

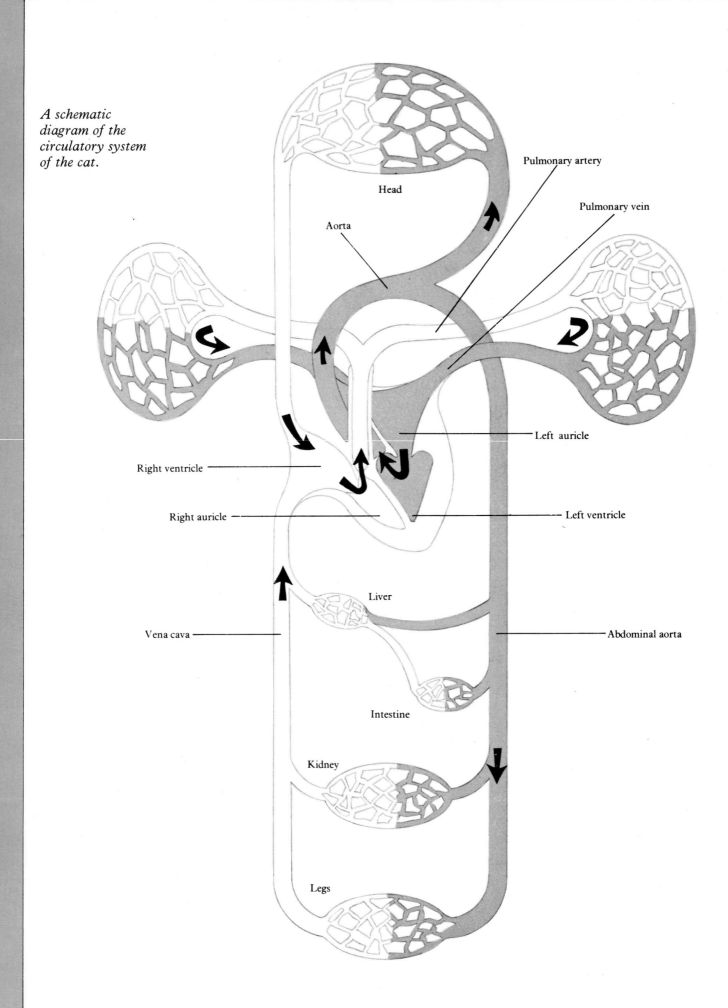

A schematic diagram of the circulatory system of the cat.

Head

Pulmonary artery

Pulmonary vein

Aorta

Left auricle

Right ventricle

Right auricle

Left ventricle

Liver

Vena cava

Abdominal aorta

Intestine

Kidney

Legs

Digestive System

Mouth

The cat has lips to hold food. Inside the mouth there is a rough tongue that can be used to lap up liquids or for cleaning.

Cats develop two sets of teeth; the baby teeth fall out at about five months, and the kitten may lose weight or even run a fever while its adult teeth are growing in. Cats do not often have cavities, but they are prone to gum trouble.

Other Digestive Organs

The cat's esophagus, stomach, intestines, liver, pancreas, and excretory systems function in much the same way as in humans.

Reproductive System

Male cats reach sexual maturity at about eleven months; most females mature between six and twelve months although females have been known to become pregnant as early as four months. Some breeds mature much faster than others.

Female Reproductive System

The *vulva*, or lips of the vagina, can be seen just below the anus. The *vagina* is the passageway connecting the external and internal parts of the system. Internally, the reproductive system functions much as it does in humans; eggs (*ova*) are formed in two ovaries; when the queen is mated the ova travel down two *Fallopian tubes* into the *uterus* where they are fertilized and the kittens develop.

Like humans and other mammals, female cats are only fertile at periodic intervals, during their *estrous cycle*. Unlike humans, however, cats are not sexually active during their *anestrous* stage. In addition cats do not ovulate until copulation is taking place, and a female can become pregnant by several toms at the same time although this is not usual as female cats do show preference when accepting a mate.

Male Reproductive System

The unaltered tomcat usually has two *testicles* suspended outside the body in the *scrotum*, to manufacture sperm. The tip of the *penis* is covered with tiny barbs, but it is not known what part they play, if any, in the mating process. The seminal fluid is manufactured by the *prostate gland*.

What sex is it?

Many people have very definite ideas about whether they want a male or a female kitten (see Choosing your Cat, page 210).

To discover a cat's sex, lift the tail gently. Female cats will have two openings that form what looks like the letter 'i' – the vertical slit below is the vulva and the small round dot above is the anus. Males have two round openings: the anus and, beneath it, the tip of the penis. The testicles, between the anus and penis, cannot be seen on kittens, though they can often be seen and felt on older cats.

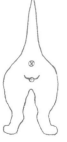
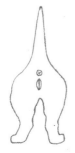

Above
A lilac Siamese with her kittens.

Left
Determining the sex of kittens –
Left : male
Right : female.

Catalog

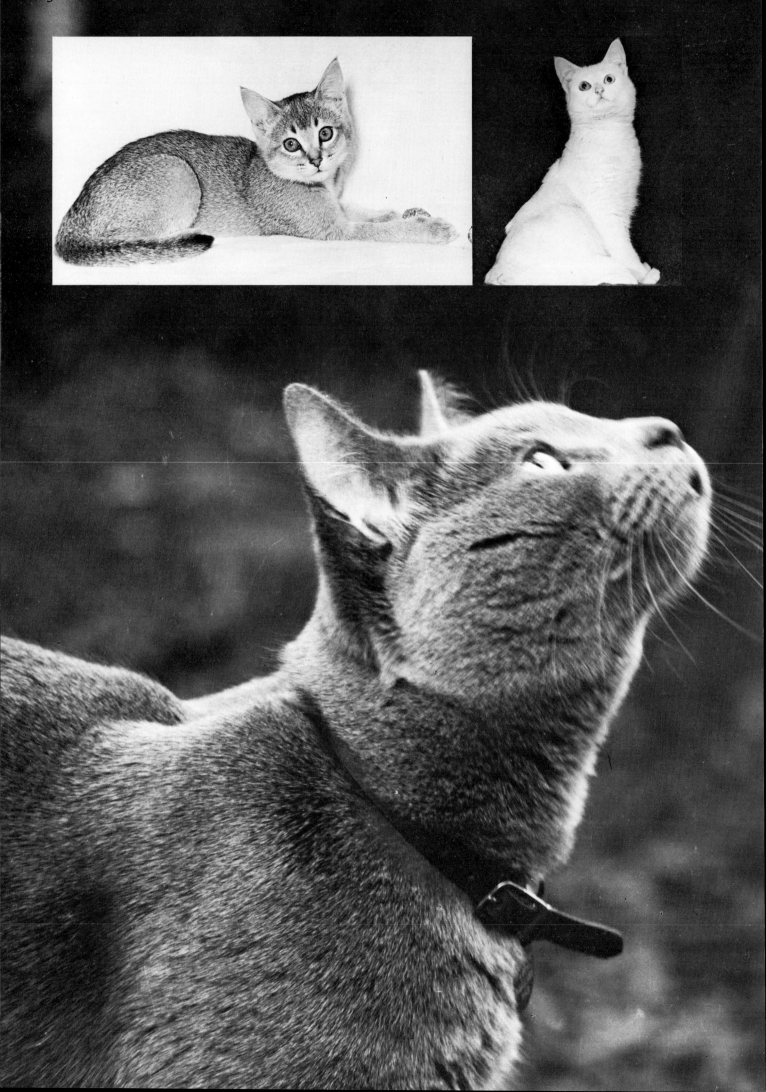

Colors and Patterns

Most show cats must meet very stringent requirements regarding color and pattern. The descriptions below are adapted from the standards prescribed by the Cat Fanciers' Association, Incorporated (CFA), the largest cat registering organization in the world.

Spectrum A

(a) *Solid Colors*

Black
The coat must be dense and coal-black from the roots to the tip, with no rusty patches or pale undercoat. Nose leather must be black and paw pads should be black or brown. Eyes should be copper.

Blue
Blue is really a shade of gray. Coat color must be level in tone from nose to tip of tail and from roots to tips of hair. Although the lighter shade (lavender gray) is preferred, a sound darker shade is better than an unsound lighter shade. Nose leather and paw pads should be blue. Eyes should be copper.

Cream
The coat must be an even, buff cream without markings, sound to the roots. Lighter shades are preferable. Nose leather and paw pads should be pink and the eyes copper.

Red
The coat must be a clear, rich red without shading, marking, or tipping and should be even from lips and chin to tail. Nose leather and paw pads should be brick-red and eyes should be copper.

White
The coat should be pure white with no yellowish patches. Nose leather and paw pads should be pink. Eyes can be blue, copper, or one of each. In this last case, the depth of color must be of equal intensity.

(b) *Shaded*

Chinchilla Silver
The undercoat should be pure white with the fur on the head, back, flanks and tail delicately tipped with black giving a silvery appearance. The cat's chin, ear tufts, chest and stomach should be pure white although the legs may be slightly shaded. Eyes, lips and nose are outlined in black. Nose leather should be brick-red and paw pads black. Eyes should be green or blue-green.

Shaded Cameo or *Red Shaded*
The undercoat should be white with red tipping, shading down like a mantle from face, sides and tail, from dark on ridge to white on chin, chest, stomach and under the tail. The legs should be the same tone as the face. The general effect is much redder than the Shell Cameo. Nose leather and paw pads must be rose-colored and eyes should be outlined in rose and copper-colored.

Shaded Silver
The undercoat should be white with black tipping shading down like a mantle from face, sides and tail, from dark on the ridge to white on the chin, chest, stomach and under the tail. The general effect is of pewter rather than the silver of the Chinchilla Cameo. Eyes, lips and nose are rimmed in black. Nose leather should be rich red color and paw pads should be black. Eyes must be green or blue-green.

Shell Cameo or *Red Chinchilla*
The undercoat should be white with the fur on the head, back, flanks and tail lightly tipped with red to give a sparkling appearance. Chin, ear tufts, stomach and chest must be white, but face and legs can be very lightly shaded. Nose leather and paw pads should be rose-colored and the copper eyes should be rose-rimmed.

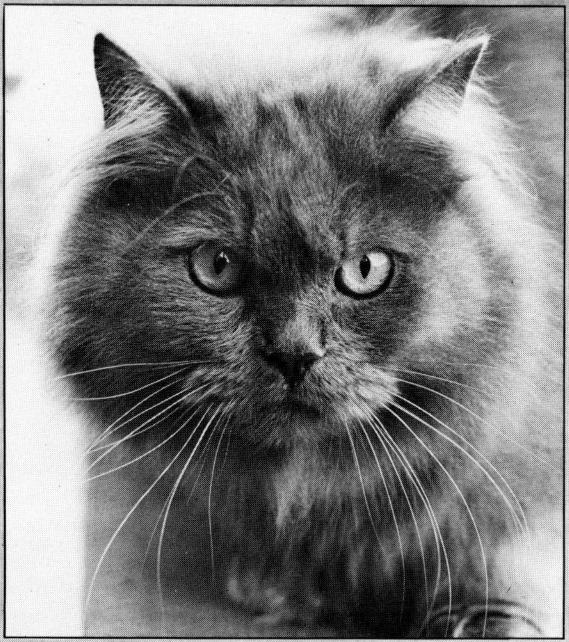

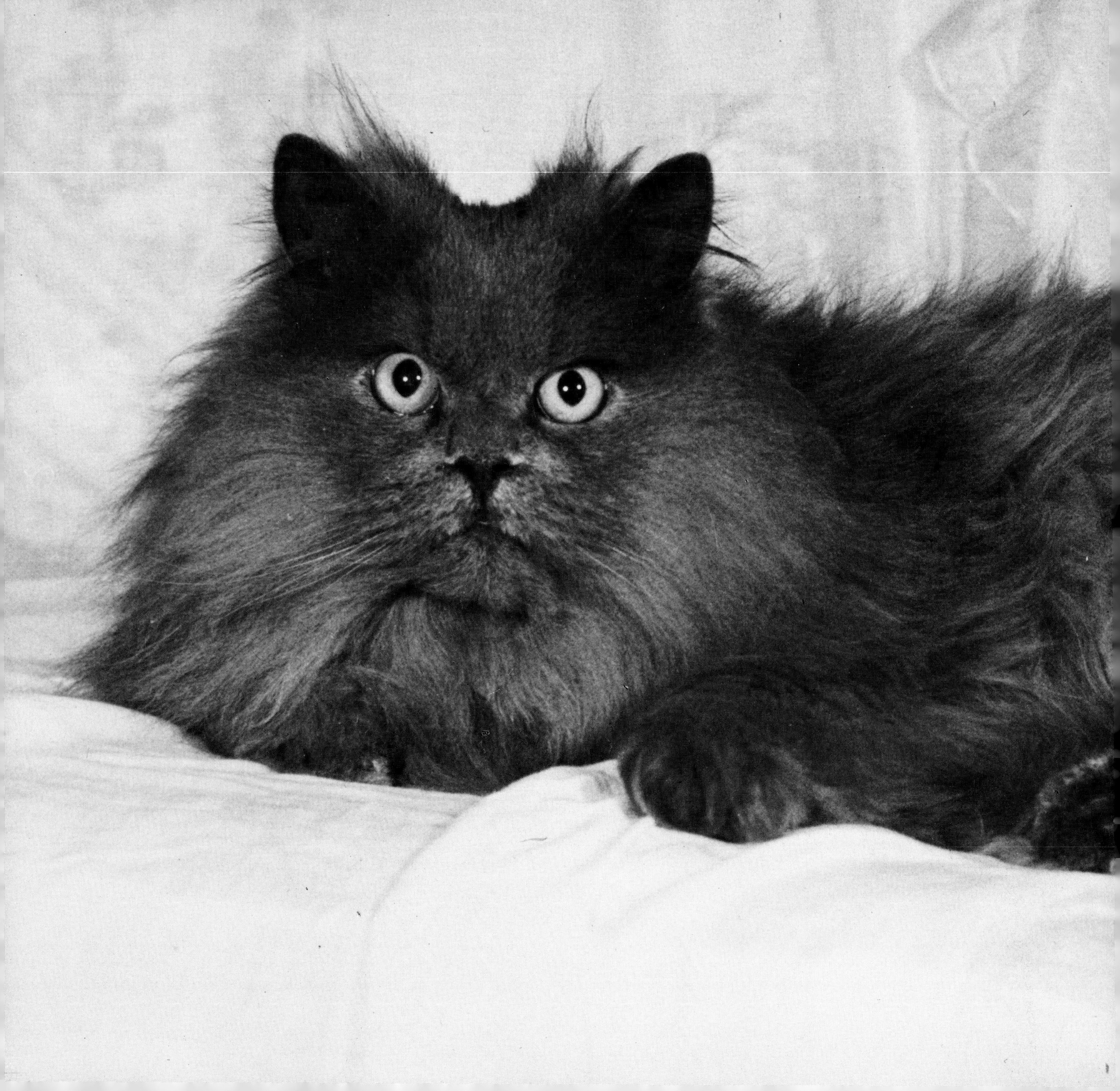

(c) Smoke

Black Smoke
The undercoat should be white with deep black tipping. Motionless, the cat appears solid black, but the white undercoat shows when it moves. Points and mask should be black except for a narrow band of white at the base of each hair which can be seen when the hairs are parted. Ruff and ear tufts should be light silver. Nose leather and paw pads must be black and the eyes, copper.

Blue Smoke
The undercoat must be white with deep blue tipping. Motionless, the cat appears solid blue but the white undercoat shows when it moves. Points and mask are blue except for a narrow band of white at the base of each hair which can be seen when the hairs are parted. The ruff and ear tufts should be white, the nose leather and paw pads should be blue and the eyes, copper.

Red Smoke
The undercoat should be white with deep red tipping. Motionless, the cat appears solid red but the white undercoat shows when it moves. Points and mask are red except for a narrow band of white at the base of each hair which can be seen when the hairs are parted. Eyes are rose-rimmed and golden in color. Nose leather and paw pads are rose.

Far left inset and left : Smokes are among the most beautiful of long-haired cats.

Above: The Silver Spotted Short-hair is not to be mistaken for the Tabby although both are equally prized.
Far right: Silver Tabby Short-hair.
Below: Brown Tabby Long-hair.

(d) *Tabbies*

The American CFA recognizes two tabby patterns: classical and mackerel. In England, they are treated as one class.

Classic Tabby Pattern

The classic tabby pattern is composed of the following elements in a dense, clearly defined color on a contrasting ground.

The legs must be ringed with 'bracelets' coming up to the body and the tail must have even rings on it as well. Several unbroken 'necklaces' must be visible on the neck and chest (the more the better). Frown marks form an intricate 'M' on the forehead. Swirls must be present on the cheeks and an unbroken line should run back from the outer corner of the eye. Vertical lines on the head should run back to the shoulder markings. Shoulder markings in the shape of a butterfly with both upper and lower wings outlined and with dots on the wings must be clearly visible. A vertical line should run down the spine from the butterfly to the tail with parallel vertical lines on either side (called 'spinals'). The three lines should be well-separated by strips of the ground color. A bulls-eye (a large blotch surrounded by two or more unbroken rings) should appear on each side. The two bulls-eyes should be identical. A double, vertical line of spots, or 'buttons' should run along the chest and stomach.

Mackerel Tabby Pattern

In many respects the markings are similar to the classic tabby pattern. Although the lines are much narrower, they must still be dense and clearly defined. As in the classic pattern there are 'bracelets' on the legs, rings on the tail, 'necklaces' on the neck and chest and an 'M' on the forehead with unbroken lines running back from the eyes and from the head to the shoulders. However, in the mackerel tabby pattern, the spine lines run together, forming a narrow saddle while narrow pencilings run around the body. The pattern on the body should look like clouds in the sky.

All tabby colors outlined below appear in both classic and mackerel patterns.

Blue Tabby

The pale ivory ground color of the coat has deep blue markings with fawn overtones or 'patina' appearing over the entire coat. Nose leather is dusty rose and paw pads are rose-colored. Eyes are copper.

Brown Tabby

The copper-brown ground color has dense black markings and the lips and chin should be the same color as the rings around the eyes. The back of the leg is black from paw to heel. Nose leather is brick-red and paw pads should be black or brown. Eyes should be copper.

Cameo Tabby

The ground color should be off-white with red markings. Nose leather and paw pads should be rose-red and eyes, copper.

Cream Tabby

The ground color should be very pale cream with buff or cream markings that are dark enough for good contrast. Nose leather and paw pads should be pink and the eyes, copper.

Red Tabby

The ground color should be red with deep red markings. The cat should have brick-red nose leather, pink paw pads and copper eyes.

Silver Tabby

The ground color should be pale, clear silver with dense black markings. The cat should have brick-red nose leather, black paw pads and green or hazel eyes.

(e) Parti-colors

Bi-color
The coat of a Bi-colored cat should be black, blue, cream or red with white feet, legs, underparts, chest and muzzle. White under the tail and around the neck is acceptable and a blaze on the face in the form of an inverted 'V' is desirable. Eyes should be copper.

Blue-Cream
In this case the coat should be blue with clearly defined, well-broken patches of cream on the body, legs, tail and head. Paler shades are preferred. Eyes should be copper. (Note: In Britain and on the Continent, the colors should be softly intermingled with no distinct patches for a shot-silk effect that is especially effective on long-haired cats. This standard is very difficult to attain.)

Calico
Here the coat should be white with well-defined, unbrindled patches of red and black. White predominates on the under-parts. Eyes should be copper. (Small red and black spots on white are character-istics of the unrecognized Harlequin.)

Dilute Calico
The coat should be white with well-defined, unbrindled patches of blue and cream; white predominates on the under-parts. Eyes should be copper.

Tortoiseshell (Tortie)
The coat must be black with well-defined, unbroken, distinct patches of red and cream on body, head, legs and tail. A red or cream blaze from forehead to nose is desirable. Eyes are copper.

Calico Short-hair (inset) and Persian.

46

Spectrum B

Spectrum B describes the colorpoint pattern and the four classic point colors. For other colors, see Colorpoint Shorthair.

The colorpoint pattern consists of a basic body color and a contrasting point color. The points appear on the cooler extremities of the cat, and have sometimes been called 'temperature points.'

The points, which must be well-defined, of a contrasting color, and of the same color density, are the mask, ears, feet, tail, and sex organs. There should not be any ticking or white hairs in the points.

The mask should cover the entire face, including the whisker pads, and be connected to the ears by 'tracings'; it should not, however, extend over the top of the head. Eyes are vivid blue for all colors.

Blue Point
Body is a glacial, bluish white, shading to white on the underparts. Points are blue; nose leather and paw pads are slate-blue.

Chocolate Point
Body is ivory, with no shading. Points are warm, even milk-chocolate; nose leather and paw pads are cinnamon.

Lilac Point (Frost Point)
Body is glacial white with no shading. Points are frosty gray with a pink tinge; nose leather is pale lilac and paw pads are cold pink. [Note: In Britain the standard calls for an off-white body with shading to the back that is the color of the points. Points are pinkish gray. Nose leather and paw pads must be faded lilac.]

Seal Point
Body is cream with warm, pale fawn shading to the back. Points are dense, dark, seal-brown; nose leather and paw pads are the same color as the points. Faults include grayness in the coat, a dark smudge on the belly or throat, white toes, or brindling in the points.

Top left, inset: The ever popular Siamese Seal Point.
Bottom left, inset: Tabby Point or Lynx Point Siamese.
Top right, inset: Seal Point Himalayan or Colorpoint.
Left: The Balinese is Foreign or Oriental in type but has long hair. It should not be mistaken for the Himalayan which is Persian in type.

Encyclopedia of Cats

Below : Siamese kitten.
Far right : Portrait of a Cheetah.

Abyssinian

The Abyssinian (or 'Aby') is sometimes called the cat from the Blue Nile (Abyssinia is present-day Ethiopia) and has long been thought to resemble the sacred cats of ancient Egypt. It is believed to have arrived in England in 1868; in 1909 it was brought to America, where it quickly became very popular.

Abyssinians – affectionate, highly intelligent cats with small, melodious voices – make delightful pets. They are happy, busy animals that dislike close confinement and always take a keen interest in their surroundings.

With its medium-sized, well-muscled, short-haired body, the Abyssinian is perhaps the most feral-looking of all the domestic breeds. The shape of its body is Oriental, like that of the Siamese, but not as long. It is slender, lithe, and graceful, with a fairly long tapering tail, slender legs and neat oval feet.

The head is a rounded, medium, well-proportioned wedge with longish ears that are broad at the base and sharp at the tip. Eyes are large, almond-shaped, and very expressive.

Abyssinians have very soft, dense, resiliant coats. Two colors – Ruddy (the most common) and Red – are recognized by cat fanciers; a Cream Abyssinian has been bred but has not yet achieved recognition.

A long-haired Abyssinian, the *Somali*, has been recognized as a breed, but is not accepted for show competition.

Ruddy Abyssinian
The coat of the Ruddy Abyssinian is reddish brown with each hair ticked with two or three shades of black or dark brown. The undercoat next to the skin is ruddy, with the outer tips of the hairs being the darkest shade. Fur on the stomach and the inside of the forelegs is a lighter shade that harmonizes with the overall body color; the back of the hind legs is black and the chin is often white. Eyes are gold or green (sometimes hazel), the nose is red, and paw pads are black or brown.

Red Abyssinian
This breed's coat is a rich, warm, coppery-red, ticked with chocolate brown. Deeper shades of red are preferable.

Acinonyx
See Cheetah

African Lion
See Lion

African Wild Cat
Felis libyca

The African Wild Cat, also known as the Bush Cat, ranges throughout Africa, in the Middle East as far north as Syria, and as far east as India. The species has also been found on Crete, Sardinia, Corsica, and Majorca. It prefers lightly forested terrain, avoiding deserts and jungle.

Usually a nocturnal hunter, it will often venture out on cool, cloudy days in search of birds or small mammals.

There are differing reports about the appearance of the African Wild Cat, which is not surprising when one considers its wide distribution. In general, it is slightly larger than the domestic cat, with mackerel tabby (see Colors and Patterns) markings. These markings are lighter than those of the domestic cat. Ears are reddish at the back and underparts of the body are yellowish. The tail is longer and more tapering than that of the European Wild Cat, but has the same distinctive rings.

American Blue
See American Short-hair; Russian Blue

American Short-hair

Once called simply the domestic short-hair, this all-American cat traveled to the New World on the *Mayflower*, and has been an integral part of American life ever since. It is a working cat – a solid citizen, a good companion, and infinitely adaptable – that now has a full pedigree from the Cat Fanciers' Association (CFA).

Although the American Short-hair developed from the same stock as the British Short-hair and is still very similar, several differences have emerged. The American Short-hair is a well-built cat with the well-developed, rippling muscles and latent power of the trained athlete. It has a powerful medium-to-large body with heavy shoulders and a well-developed chest, firm strong legs of medium length, and a medium-length tail that tapers from a thick base and ends bluntly.

The head is large and well-proportioned, slightly longer than it is wide. The muzzle is square, the chin firm, the cheeks full and the nose medium (snub noses are considered faults). The medium size, wide-set ears are slightly rounded. Eyes are large and round, set well apart, and slant slightly at the outer edge. They should be bright, clear, and alert.

The American Short-hair conformation covers a wide range of breeds, including the Chinchilla and Shaded Silver. It is recognized in all colors and patterns of Spectrum A (see Colors and Patterns).

Andean Cat
See Mountain Cat

Angora

Angora (now called Ankara, the capital of Turkey) is thought to have been the home of the first long-haired cats seen in Europe. Cross-breeding and a preference for the Persian type virtually eliminated the breed in Europe, and only a few Angoras remained in Turkey. There they were deeply appreciated but they were not known elsewhere.

Turkish authorities eventually realized that the breed was in danger of total extinction and began a small breeding program. In 1962 and again in 1966, Colonel Walter Grant of the US Army was able, through his friendship with zoo officials, to bring two unrelated pairs of Angoras to the United States. The imports aroused a new interest among breeders and in 1970 the Cat Fanciers' Association recognized the Turkish Angora as a separate breed, establishing a provisional standard. They have still not been recognized in Britain.

Right : American Short-hair.
Below : Abyssinian kitten. In the past these cats were known as 'Bunny' or 'Rabbit' cats because of their ticked fur.

The Angora is slightly smaller than medium in size with a small head and tapering, upright ears. The eyes are large, almond-shaped, slightly slanted, and wide-set; they can be either blue, amber, or one of each color (some blue-eyed Angoras suffer from deafness). The tail is long, full, and tapering, and should not be kinked. When the cat is relaxed and moving it carries its tail horizontally over its body, almost touching the ears. Paw pads, nose leather, and lips are pink.

The coat should be fine, medium length, and soft with a silky finish. There are tufts of hair between the toes. Only white Angoras are presently eligible for the CFA Championship competition, though they have been bred in other colors from Spectrum A (see Colors and Patterns).

The Turkish Government and the Ankara Zoo deserve great credit for their work in saving this very special cat from extinction.

Archangel

See Maltese; Russian Blue

Balinese

The Balinese is basically a long-haired Siamese. The mutation appeared in America in litters of purebred Siamese and it was found that when the mutations were mated they bred true. In other words, a Balinese can only be produced now by mating one Balinese with another. They

Balinese cat and her kitten.

were recognized as a breed in the United States in 1963 and in the UK in 1974.

Balinese have voices and characters similar to Siamese cats, but are considered by some to be less demanding. Like the Siamese, too, they are highly intelligent and very affectionate animals.

Balinese cats should not be confused with Persians or Himalayans, which have much longer coats. The coat on a Balinese is soft, silky, and about two inches long, requiring much less attention than that of other long-haired cats.

The Balinese body is tight, slim, and elegant, with fine bones and firm muscles. Balinese cats should be medium in size and the same width at the shoulders and hips. Legs are long and slim, with the hind legs longer than the front. The tail is long, thin, and tapers to a point; the tail hair spreads out like a plume.

The head is a long, tapering wedge that starts from the nose and flares out to the ears in straight lines. In profile, the slope from the top of the head to the tip of the nose is a long, straight line. Ears are very large and pointed, and continue the lines of the wedge. Eyes are medium-sized and almond-shaped, of a deep, vivid blue. They should never be crossed. Balinese have fairly long necks.

The Balinese falls under Spectrum B (see Colors and Patterns). Points and mask should be clearly defined without brindling or white hairs. The whole face should be covered by the mask. The coat will probably darken as the cat gets older, but the shading should remain even.

Bay Lynx
See Bobcat

56

Bengal Tiger
See Tiger

Bi-colored Long-hair
See Bi-colored Persian; Colors and Patterns

Bi-colored Persian
The Bi-colored Persian (often called Parti-colored Persian) was originally shown only in black and white and entered under the name Magpie. Later it was entered under the 'Any Other Color' classification. It was recognized as a separate breed in the mid-1960s. Bi-colored Persians are important in breeding long-haired Calico Cats.

Conformation should be that of the Persian: big, cobby body with short thick legs, round broad head and short bushy tail (see also Persian).

The coat should be long, flowing, and silky. It must combine white with one other solid color; tabby markings are considered faults. (See also Colors and Patterns)

Bi-colored Persian.

Bi-colored Short-hair
See Colors and Patterns

Birman

According to legend the Birman, also known as the Sacred Cat of Burma, guarded the temples in that country in ancient times. Even today they are treated with reverence in Burma, since many people believe that they are reincarnations of Burmese priests who will, when they die, carry the priests' souls to paradise.

Birmans were introduced into France in 1919, but nearly disappeared during the Second World War. Enough were saved, however, to ensure the preservation of the breed after the war. They were recognized as a separate breed in 1966 in Britain and in 1967 in the United States. They are gaining rapidly in popularity, partly because of their beauty and partly because of their intelligence and affectionate nature.

The Birman has a long body with medium-length, heavy legs; large, round, firm paws; and a medium-length, bushy tail. The head is wide and rounded with full cheeks, and is slightly flat above the eyes. Ears and nose are medium in length. Eyes are almost round, and of a bright china blue.

The golden beige coat is long and silky, with a heavy ruff around the neck, and slightly curly hair on the belly. The coat does not mat, making Birmans extremely easy to care for.

Birman coloring falls under Spectrum B (see Colors and Patterns) except for the feet, which are tipped with white like a glove. On the front paws these gloves should end in an even line at the third joint; on the back they cover the entire paw, ending in a point that goes up the back of the hock like a gauntlet. These points are often called 'the laces.'

Birman adult and kitten (inset).

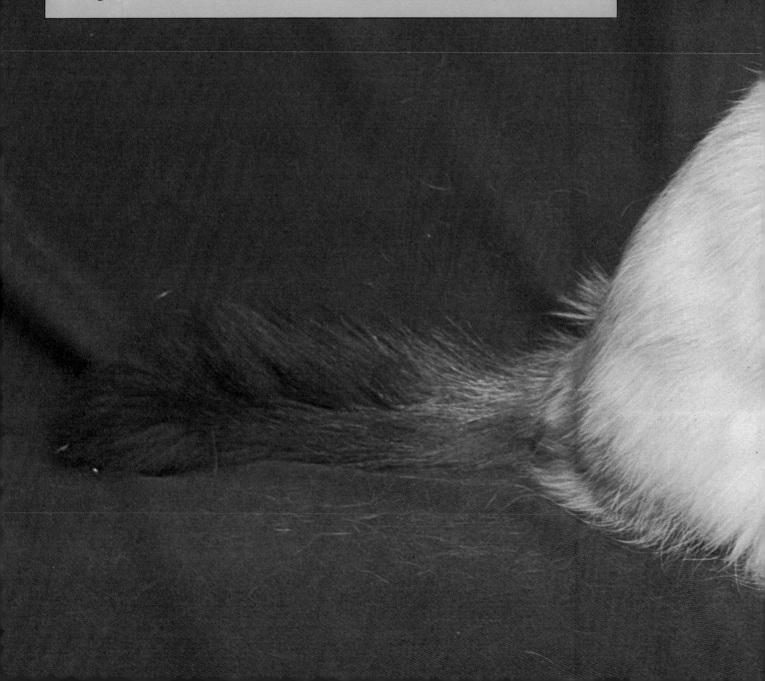

Black Long-hair

See Black Persian

Black-footed Cat

Felis nigripes

The Black-footed Cat is now very rare even in its habitat in Africa which includes the Kalahari Desert, Botswana, and parts of the Orange Free State and the Transvaal.

It is a nocturnal hunter, preying on birds, lizards, and the like.

Slightly smaller than the domestic cat, it has a pale brown coat with a white underbody and indistinct spots which darken and merge together toward the legs to form three rings. The soles of its feet are black (a characteristic also of domestic tabbies).

The Black-footed Cat has successfully crossbred with domestic cats, but such breeding is not a common occurrence.

Black Panther

See Leopard

Black Persian

Although the Black Persian (or Black Long-hair, as it is known in Britain) is one of the oldest pedigree colors known, the numbers being shown are not increasing because it is so difficult to obtain a perfect, jet-black coat.

Not only are coats often marked by occasional white hairs and bands which show up under lights, but the coats require constant attention and grooming to prevent their being marked by sunshine or rain. The coats do not become dense and shiny until the cat is a year to a year and a half old, and the rusty or gray appearance of the kittens often discourages would-be breeders.

Black Persians are useful for breeding Tortoiseshells, Whites, and Bi-colors. (See also Colors and Patterns; Persian)

Black Short-hair

This is the cat associated with the devil and witchcraft in more superstitious times. Today black cats are still regarded with lingering misgivings in America and Ireland, but in Britain they have come to be thought of as lucky cats.

A pedigree Black conforms to the standards for its body type (see American Short-hair and British Short-hair), with orange or deep copper-colored eyes and shiny, glossy, jet-black fur. As with black long-haired cats, short coats suffer from excessive sun or damp, and constant grooming is necessary to avoid rusty patches. Hand grooming with a chamois leather is an excellent way to remove grease and leaves a beautiful sheen.

A close-up and a full portrait of the Black Short-hair.

Black Smoke Short-hair
See Smoke Short-hair

Blue American Short-hair
See American Short-hair; Russian Blue

Blue Burmese
See Burmese

Blue Chinchilla
See Chinchilla

Blue Cream Burmese
See Burmese

Blue Cream Long-hair
See Blue Cream Persian

Blue Cream Persian

Blue Cream Persians are very attractive cats, produced by mating Blues and Creams. Males are rare and are always sterile. Body should conform to that of the Persian (see Persian); eyes should be large, round, and of a copper or dark orange color. (See also Colors and Patterns)

Blue Cream Point
See Colorpoint Short-hair; Himalayan

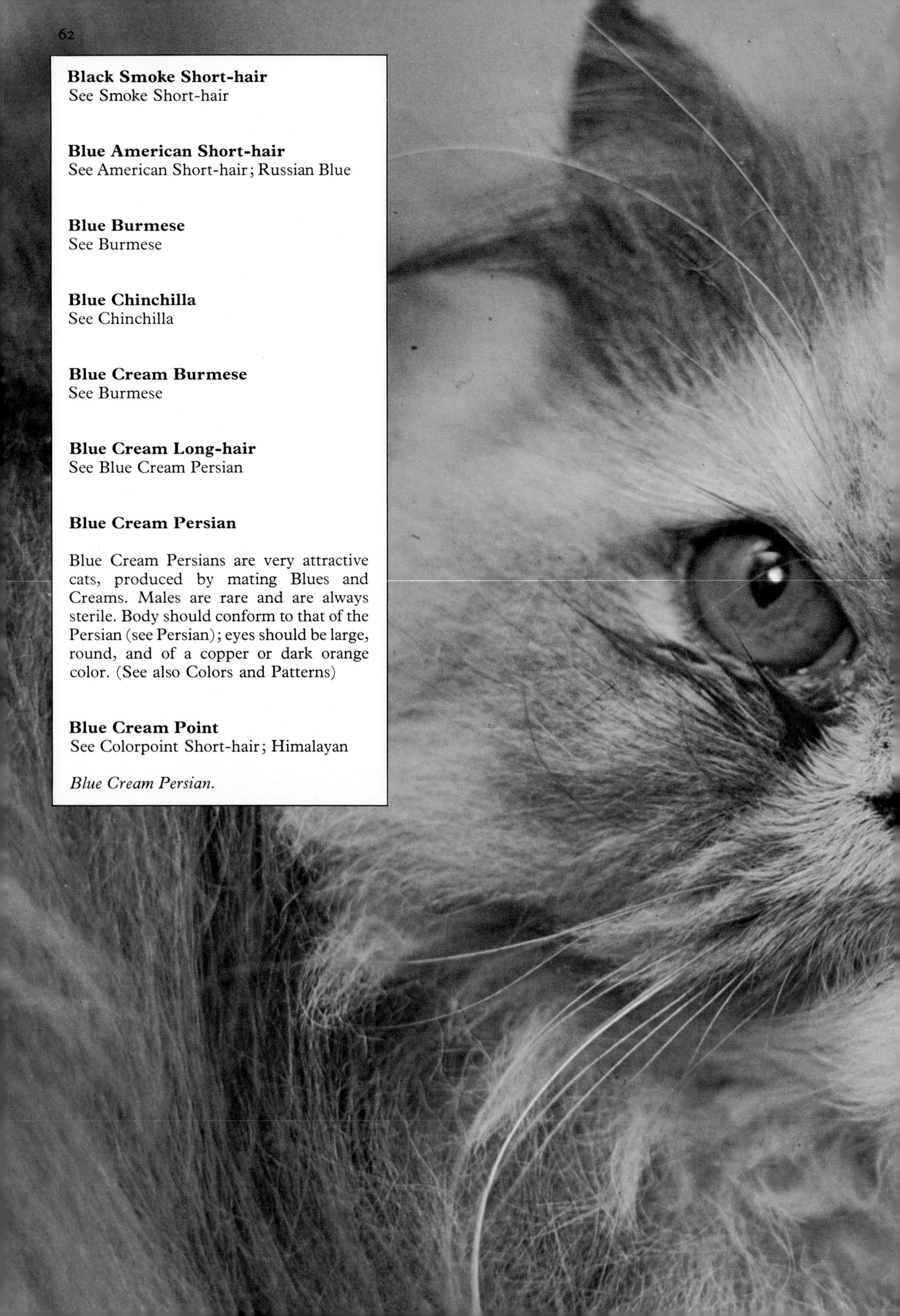

Blue Cream Persian.

Blue Cream Short-hair

As with the Blue Cream Persian, this variety is almost entirely female; males are always sterile. Again the type is the result of Blue and Cream matings, though it sometimes appears in Tortoiseshell litters if both parents carry blue genes.

Blue Cream Short-hairs should conform to the standards for their body type (see American Short-hair; British Short-hair; Colors and Patterns), except that eyes may only be copper, orange, or yellow.

They are very popular cats, both for their pleasant personalities and the large variety of kittens they can produce.

Blue Long-hair
See Blue Persian

Blue Lynx Point
See Colorpoint Short-hair

Blue Persian

The Blue Persian has been very important in the improved breeding of nearly all solid-color Persians and in the development of new colors such as Colorpoints. It is one of the most attractive and photogenic breeds.

Lighter shades are preferred, but evenness of color is more important than tone. White hairs in the coat, green eye rims, and kinked tails are considered faults. Kittens are often born with tabby markings, but lose these quickly as they grow up. Although this cat should have a snub nose, one that is too short indicates overbreeding. The head should be broad, the ears small, the eyes round and copper-colored, and the ruff large and well-developed.

Far right: Blue Persian (or Blue Long-hair as it is called in Great Britain). Below: This Blue Colorpoint kitten is usually called a Blue Point Himalayan although both names are acceptable. (See page 126.) Overleaf: A hungry Bobcat takes its kill to its lair deep in the forest.

Mating a Blue male with a Cream female can produce Cream males and Blue Cream females; litters from Blue males and Blue Cream females can include Blue and Cream males and Blue and Blue Cream females; Blue females mated to Cream males can have Blue males and Blue Cream females.

Blue Point
See Colors and Patterns; Himalayan; Siamese

Blue Russian
See Maltese; Russian Blue

Blue Short-hair

There are several recognized breeds of Blue Short-hairs. Each breed has certain characteristics which set it apart from the others (for example, each has differently colored eyes). If a cat is of poor quality, however, these distinctions become blurred and even experts cannot always be sure of the actual breed.

Recognized breeds of Blue Short-hairs are:
Blue American Short-hair
Blue Burmese
Blue Exotic Short-hair
Blue Japanese Bobtail
Blue Manx 'Longie'
Blue Oriental Short-hair
British Blue
Chartreux
Korat
Maltese
Russian Blue

Blue Smoke Persian
See Smoke Persian; Colors and Patterns

Blue Smoke Short-hair
See Smoke Short-hair

Blue Tabby
See Colors and Patterns; Tabby

Blue Tortie Point
See Colorpoint Short-hair

Blue Tortoiseshell and White
See Colors and Patterns (Dilute Calico); Calico (Dilute Calico).

Bobcat
felis rufa

The Bobcat is also known as the Bay Lynx and is closely related to, but smaller than, the Northern Lynx.

It ranges over a large area in North America from southern Canada to south Mexico, preferring open ground, but is able to adapt to many other habitats. Its diet consists mainly of birds and small mammals but it has been known to kill poultry, sheep, calves, and even deer. Its pelt is of little value, but it is often hunted for sport.

The Bobcat's coat is spotted and colored a rusty brown on the back, graduating to creamy white underneath. This coloring applies to the tail also – an important way to differentiate the Bobcat from the Lynx is by the size of its tail. Bobcats with pale brown fur have also been sighted, and the size and pattern of the spots can vary a great deal.

Size of the animal varies from 32 to 50 inches for males and from 28 to 48 inches for females. Litters contain up to four kittens.

Bobtail
See Japanese Bobtail

Bombay

This shiny black hybrid is a recent addition to the show scene. It was originally produced by mating American Short-

A Bobcat (or Bay Lynx) chases a deermouse in the snow in the mountains of Colorado.
Inset, far right: The Bobcat's coloring allows it to blend into its environment with ease.

hairs and Burmese, and has been called 'the cat with the patent leather coat and copper penny eyes.'

The standards for body type are almost exactly the same as those for the Burmese: a medium-size, muscular body with legs in proportion and a straight, medium-length tail; a round head with a full face and short, well-developed muzzle; alert, wide-set ears that are medium in size, broad at the base, and slightly rounded at the tips; and round, wide-set eyes.

In judging, 55 percent of the Bombay Standard is concerned with coat and color – more than any other breed. The coat must be fine, short, and satiny, and lie very close to produce that 'patent leather' sheen. Fur must be black to the roots. Nose leather and paw pads are black. Eye color ranges from yellow to deep copper (never green).

British Blue

The British Blue is probably one of the most popular short-hairs in the United Kingdom, largely because of its gentle, placid disposition, affectionate nature and high intelligence. The females make excellent mothers.

Blues conform very closely to British Short-hair standards, but their coats are more plush. The color of the coat can vary from light to medium blue, but it must be even, with no white hairs.

The British Blue is essentially the same as the Exotic Short-hair (blue) in America and the Chartreux in Europe. It is recognized as a separate breed in the United States, but is not accepted for CFA show competition.

British Cream
See Cream Short-hair

British Short-hair

The British Short-hair is similar to its American cousin, but has slightly different standards: shorter legs and tail, smaller ears, and rounder head and eyes. The coat should be fine and soft, but not wooly.

British Short-hairs are not currently accepted for show competition by the American CFA.

Right: The white British Short-hair is similar in most respects to the American Short-hair: the British nose is slightly smaller and the coat more plush.

72

Bronze Mau
See Egyptian Mau

Brown Burmese
See Burmese (Sable)

Brown Tabby
See Colors and Patterns; Tabby

Sable or Brown Burmese.

Burmese

Burmese (called Zibelines in France) were developed in the United States and can be traced back to a single female (probably a Siamese hybrid) named Wong Mau. Wong Mau arrived in New Orleans in 1930 in the company of a sailor. She was eventually given to Dr Joseph C Thompson of San Francisco who decided to try to continue this sable brown breed.

An experimental breeding program was established with the help of cat geneticists and breeders, and despite many problems – lack of a brown male and Wong Mau's own mixed ancestry – the breed we know today was evolved.

Burmese are hardy, sociable cats that make excellent companions and tend to be very possessive about 'their' families.

The Burmese is a medium-size cat with heavier bones and more muscle than its size would indicate; a round, strong chest; and a straight back. Legs are slender and in good proportion to the body; hind legs are longer than front legs. Paws are round. The tail is medium, slender, and straight.

The head is round, with a blunt wedge-shaped muzzle and a full face. There is a strong lower jaw and a distinct nose break. Ears are medium in size, broad at the base and slightly rounded at the tip; they are wide-set and tip slightly forward. The wide-set eyes are a rounded almond shape.

Sable (or 'Brown') Burmese is the only color recognized by the CFA in America, and to the purist a solid-color, satin-sheen, sable brown will probably always be the only proper color for the breed. Because of its hybrid ancestry, however, other colors have emerged; blue, champagne, and platinum are the most common, and have been recognized by other organizations. In England, especially, other colors are very popular and are encouraged.

Right : The ever-popular Blue Burmese.
Below : This Siamese kitten is similar in type to the Burmese but with a less solid body and more pointed face.

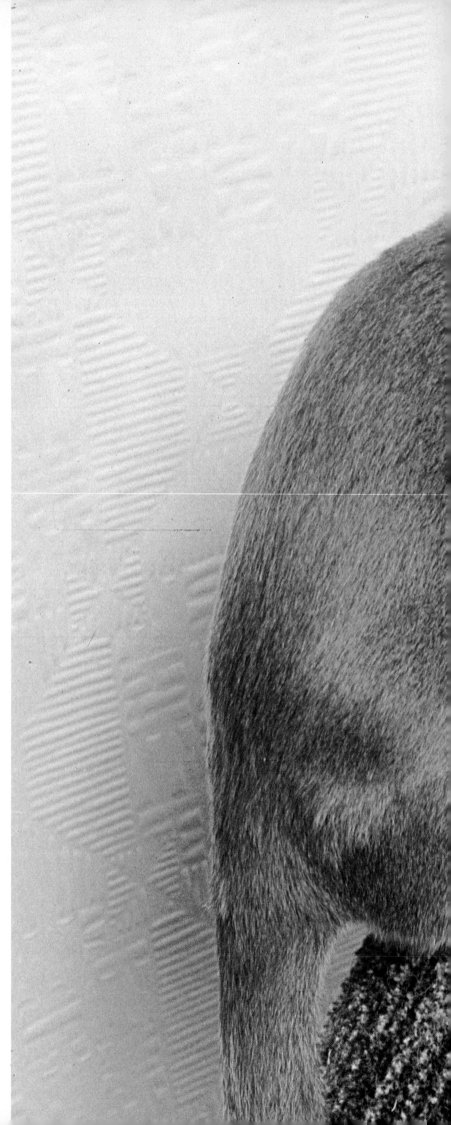

The two most popular types of Burmese cats : on the left is a Sable or Brown Burmese and on the right is a Blue Burmese. Depending on the genealogy of the cats involved both colors can occur in the same litter as can any of the other varieties of Burmese cats.

Blue Burmese
This color was achieved by mating the lighter-colored kittens from a Sable Burmese litter, and the required conformation is the same as for the Sable Burmese. The coat should be a bluish-gray with a silvery tinge on face, ears, and feet; the back and tail are slightly darker. Eyes are yellow; they can have a slight greenish tinge, but should never be a distinct green. Paw pads are gray and nose leather is dark gray. Kittens have tabby markings which fade.

Blue Cream Burmese
This is a female-only type, with the standard Burmese conformation. This color is popular in Britain, where the standard for Blue Creams calls for a smooth mixture of the two colors. (See Colors and Patterns.) Nose leather and paw pads are blotched blue and pink.

Brown Burmese
See Sable Burmese

Champagne Burmese
This is a very popular color, called Chocolate in the United Kingdom. The coat should be a warm, even, milk-chocolate color; ears and mask can be slightly darker. Paw pads are slightly redder and nose leather slightly browner than the coat.

Champagne Tortie Burmese
Recognized only in Britain, this variety should be a mixture of chocolate and

Above : Blue Burmese.

cream, without barring. Colors may be mingled or blotched, and solid color feet, legs, and tails are acceptable. Nose leather and paw pads are chocolate and pink, and can also be plain or blotched. Adherence to Burmese conformation is important.

Chocolate Burmese
See Champagne Burmese

Cream Burmese
The Cream Burmese is a rich cream color, paler on the underparts, darker on back and tail, and darker still on the ears. Slight tabby markings on the face are accepted. Nose leather and paw pads are pink.

Lavender Burmese
See Platinum Burmese

Lilac Burmese
See Platinum Burmese

Platinum Burmese
The Platinum (or Lilac) Burmese was only recently recognized in Britain. The coat should be dove gray with a frosted, pinkish sheen, slightly darker on ears and mask. Nose leather and paw pads are a lavender pink. This variety results from mating two Champagne Burmese that carry a blue gene, or a Champagne and a Blue.

Platinum Tortie Burmese
The colors, platinum and cream, should be distributed without barring. Conformation is more important than coloration or markings.

Red Burmese
The coat color should be a golden red, fading to tangerine on the underparts. Eyes are darker and slight tabby markings are acceptable. Nose leather and paw pads are chocolate but pink is acceptable.

Sable Burmese
The Sable Burmese has a close-lying, satin-textured coat of a deep, rich, warm sable brown that gradually becomes slightly lighter on the underparts. Otherwise the color is absolutely even, with no shadings or markings. Kittens are sometimes coffee-colored, with shadow markings and a few white hairs. Nose leather and paw pads are brown. Eyes should range from yellow to gold; green eyes are considered faults and blue eyes disqualify the cat on the show bench – as do kinked tails or white spots in the coat.

Tortoiseshell Burmese
This is a female-only type. Burmese conformation is more important than coat color, which is a mingled or blotched mixture of brown, cream, and red. Legs and tail are often a solid color. Nose leather and paw pads are plain or blotched, chocolate or pink.

Right : The Oriental or Foreign Short-hair is similar in configuration to the Siamese but has the colorpoints eliminated. The cat here is an Oriental or Foreign Smoke, a breed not yet recognized. (See page 158 for further information.) Below : Oriental Lavender Queen and kittens.

Bush Cat
See African Wild Cat

Caffre Cat
See African Wild Cat

Calico Cat

Calico cats come in both long- and short-haired varieties (called Tortoiseshell and White Long-hair and Short-hair in the United Kingdom). The Calico Short-hair is believed to have originated in Spain, and is one of the earliest known varieties.

The Calico is a difficult cat to reproduce since it is an almost all-female type. A Black or White male makes the best stud, but breeding is a chancy matter at best. Care should be taken to avoid mating cats with white hairs or tabby markings, since these traits will often be reproduced in the kittens.

Conformation and coat quality should be that of the appropriate Persian or Short-hair standard.

Coloration requirements vary from association to association on both sides of the Atlantic. In America the CFA and most other associations call for predominantly white underparts and black and red patches (see Colours and Patterns), but some others ask for black, red, and cream patches. The patches must always be clearly defined and free from brindling. Feet and legs, the whole underside of the body, tail, chest, and most of the neck should be white with splashes on the nose. The white should also come up to cover the lower parts of the sides. Eyes are orange- or copper-colored; hazel eyes are sometimes permitted in short-hairs.

In England the standard calls for well-distributed black, red, and cream patches interspersed with white.

Dilute Calico
Dilute Calicos were the result of mating Calicos and Blue and White Bi-coloreds. They are called Blue Tortoiseshell and White Long-hairs and Short-hairs in the United Kingdom. (See Colors and Patterns)

Right : Calico Cat.

Cameo

Cameos are attractive long-haired cats developed in America during the 1950s and recognized in 1960. They still have not gained recognition in England.

Coloration is more important than conformation which should be the same as for other Persians.

Cameos are found with shaded colors – Shell Cameo and Shaded Cameo – in Smokes, and with tabby markings (see Colors and Patterns). There is also a Tortoiseshell Cameo that is slowly gaining recognition; it has a silvery white undercoat and standard tortoiseshell markings, with ticking of red and cream or black and blue.

Tabby Cameo coats are also recognized in Exotic Short-hairs by some governing bodies.

Left : Smoke Cameo.
Below : Shaded Cameo.

Canadian Hairless
See Sphynx

Caracal Lynx
Felis caracal

This distinctive wild cat once ranged over an enormous area from south Russia and the Ukraine, through the Middle East, to north and central India and much of Africa. Now, however, it is rapidly disappearing. The Caracal likes wide-open country, usually thinly bushed or mountainous. It avoids forested regions, and is quite able to survive in semi-desert country. It hunts by bursting from cover and hurling itself upon its prey which can be as small as a hare or as large as an impala. It can also leap into the air and snatch birds as they take flight; Caracals have even been known to kill eagles. They can be trained to hunt, and have on occasion been used in packs by sportsmen in Asia.

A small (35–40 inches total length), elegant cat, the Caracal gives an impression of great strength. The coat is an even reddish-yellow on an adult; many Caracals have silver hairs, giving them a yellowish-gray appearance. The chin and underparts are white, and there are dark patches above the eyes which look almost oriental, and at the base of the whiskers. Kittens are reddish brown.

The Caracal's ears are its most distinctive feature; they are large, long, and pointed, with long black tufts. The tail is short, like that of the lynx.

Caspian Tiger
See Tiger

Central American Jaguar
See Jaguar

Champagne Burmese
See Burmese

Champagne Tortie Burmese
See Burmese

A Caracal Lynx.

Chartreux

The sturdy Chartreux is the indigenous Blue Short-hair of France, and is thought to have been brought to that country from South Africa by Carthusian monks.

It is a gentle, affectionate, and intelligent cat – and is also a skilled hunter of rodents.

Conformation and coloring are essentially the same as the British Blue.

Chat Sans Poils
See Sphynx

Cheetah

There are still two types of Cheetah: the African (*Acinonyx jubatus jubatus*) and the Asian (*A jubatus venaticus*).

At one time they were found throughout Africa and the Middle East and in large areas of Asia as far east as India. Today, however, they are rarely seen outside South Africa and a very few places in Asia. Protective legislation has been passed in North Africa, but the species is in danger of extinction there unless the laws take effect immediately. Cheetahs have not been seen on the eastern Mediterranean coast for over 100 years, and none have been reported in India for more than 20 years.

Cheetahs are the fastest animals on earth; their maximum speed (which they can only maintain for a very short time) is over 60 mph; in a sudden burst from cover they can attain 45 mph in as little as two seconds.

They inhabit open country with just enough cover to assist their hunting and enough grass to feed their prey (gazelles, other deer, hares, etc.), tending to avoid heavily forested and mountainous regions. Cheetahs hunt by both day and night. Although they are not easily trained, they adapt very well to domestication and can be used as hunting animals, often becoming very attached to their owners.

Cheetahs are long, slim, elegant animals, with bodies about 4.5 feet long and tails of

about 2.5 feet. They stand about three feet high. The head is small in relation to the body, with jaws that lack the strength of other big cats. The claws are permanently extended from the age of about ten weeks, and the paws are ridged for better traction. This, along with extraordinarily powerful hind legs and a supple back accounts for the very high speeds.

Kittens are born with smoky gray fur and a silver mane. When they are about ten weeks old the coat turns tawny; the coloring is completed with the addition of small black spots. Two heavy black stripes run from the corner of the eyes to the edge of the mouth, outlining the face and giving the animal a sad but noble expression.

The long-legged and graceful Cheetah.

Chestnut Brown Foreign
See Havana Brown

Chinchilla

This small, long-haired cat was created almost a century ago in Britain from a cross between a Silver Tabby and a Smoke; in America it is often called Silver Persian. Many consider it to be the most beautiful of the long-haired cats.

Conformation should basically be that of other long-haired varieties, except for its lighter bone structure which gives it a dainty appearance. Unfortunately this often counts against it in America, where it is expected to meet the same standard as the heavier breeds.

The head is round and broad; the snub nose has a brick-red tip; and the ears are wide-set and well-tufted. The eyes should be large, emerald or blue-green in color. The tail should be short and bushy.

The coat should be thick, long, and silky, pure white on the underparts, chin and ear tufts. All the other hairs are delicately tipped with black, giving the animal a shimmering, silvery appearance. Heavy tipping, yellow patches, or brown, cream, or tabby markings are considered faults. Kittens are born with darker fur and tabby markings which eventually disappear. (See also Colors and Patterns.)

Blue Chinchilla
This cat, the result of mating a Chinchilla with a Blue Persian, is being developed in England, but has not yet been recognized as a separate variety. The adult cat has a pure white undercoat, tipped on the back, tail, flanks, head, and ears with blue-gray. Legs may have ticking. Eyes can be orange or amber. In the UK this variety can be entered in the 'Any Other Color' class.

Chinchillas – right, below and overleaf!

Chinese Desert Cat
Felis bieti

The Chinese Desert Cat was only discovered during the 1880s, and even today very little is known about its habits.

It inhabits Mongolia, the outer provinces of China, and the Tibetan Steppes, in areas that are generally either dry grassland or semi-desert. Its diet probably consists of small mammals, reptiles, and birds.

In size it is only slightly larger than the domestic cat. Its color is grayish yellow, with white underparts and a dark-ringed tail.

Chinese Tiger
See Tiger

Chocolate Burmese
See Burmese

Chocolate Cream Point
See Colorpoint Short-hair

Chocolate Lynx Point
See Colorpoint Short-hair

Left and below : Chinchilla kittens.

Chocolate Point
See Colors and Patterns; Siamese

Chocolate Self Long-hair
See Himalayan

Chocolate Tortie Point Burmese
See Burmese

Clouded Leopard

This expert tree-climber can be found in the forests of Java, Taiwan, the Malay Peninsula, and parts of mainland China. Not much is known about its habits; it is

Above: Clouded Leopard.

said to hunt at night and its diet is assumed to include small mammals but not birds.

Males can be as large as 3.5 feet plus a one-foot tail, and weigh up to 50 pounds. Females are a foot shorter and weigh about 35 pounds. They are slender cats, with coats that vary from grayish yellow to brown. Brown blotches with clouded centers run vertically, covering the body, tail, flanks, and legs (where they give way to spots). The head and face are also spotted, and the underparts are white.

Colorpoint Long-hair
See Himalayan

Colorpoint Short-hair

The Colorpoint Short-hair is the result of the desire of breeders in America to extend the basic colorpoint pattern (see Colors and Patterns) beyond the four classic colors (Seal Point, Chocolate Point, Blue Point, and Lilac Point) to include other colors and patterns.

This was accomplished by mating Siamese and American Short-hairs, to produce a cat that retained the Siamese conformation and colorpoint factor, but acquired additional colors and patterns from the American Short-hair.

Their success is an outstanding example of the art of breeding. In addition, the Colorpoint Short-hair is a warm, friendly cat that makes an excellent pet.

The Colorpoint Short-hair should be identical to the Siamese in every respect save color (see Siamese). The cats are divided into three categories: Solid Color Point, Lynx (or Tabby) Point, and Parti-Color Point. Eyes in all cases should be deep blue.

Solid Color Point

(a) *Red Point :* Experimental breeding between Seal Point Siamese females and Red Tabby Short-hair males began during the Second World War; Red Points were recognized in America in 1956 and in England in 1966. The body should be clear white with any shading the same color as the points which are deep reddish brown. Nose leather and paw pads are flesh or coral.

(b) *Cream Point :* As above, except that the points are apricot.

Lynx Point

Also known as Silver Point Siamese, Shadow Point, and Tabby Colorpoint Short-hair. Lynx Points tend to have gentler natures than other Siamese.

In all of the colors described below, the body color may be lightly shaded. The points contain distinct, darker shaded bars separated by a lighter background color. The ears are the basic point color with a paler, thumbprint-shaped mark in the center.

(a) *Blue Lynx Point :* Cold, bluish white to platinum-gray body, shading to a lighter color on stomach and chest, with deep blue-gray points on the lighter ground. Nose leather is slate or pink, edged in slate; paw pads are slate-colored.

(b) *Chocolate Lynx Point :* Ivory body with warm mild chocolate points on lighter ground. Nose leather is cinnamon or pink, edged in cinnamon; paw pads are cinnamon.

(c) *Lilac Lynx Point :* Glacial white body and frosty gray points with a pinkish tone on a lighter ground. Nose leather is lavender pink or pink, edged in lavender pink; paw pads are lavender pink.

(d) *Red Lynx Point :* White body with deep red points on a lighter ground. Nose leather and paw pads are flesh-color or coral.

(e) *Seal Lynx Point :* Cream or pale fawn body color, with seal brown points on a lighter ground. Nose leather is seal brown or pink, edged in seal brown; paw pads are seal brown.

Parti-color Point

In all colors the points are a basic solid color mottled with patches of one or more contrasting colors. A blaze on the mask is desirable; when such a blaze is present the nose leather may be mottled.

(a) *Blue Cream Point :* Cold bluish white to platinum-gray body, lighter on chest and stomach; deep blue-gray points uniformly mottled with cream. Nose is slate-colored although flesh or coral mottling is permitted with a blaze. Paw pads are slate but flesh or coral mottling is permitted where the point color extends into the pads.

Right : Lynx Point – an excellent example of one type of Colorpoint Short-hair.
Below : This picture of a Long-haired Colorpoint or Himalayan (page 126) shows the difference in the length of fur between the Long-hair and the Short-hair.

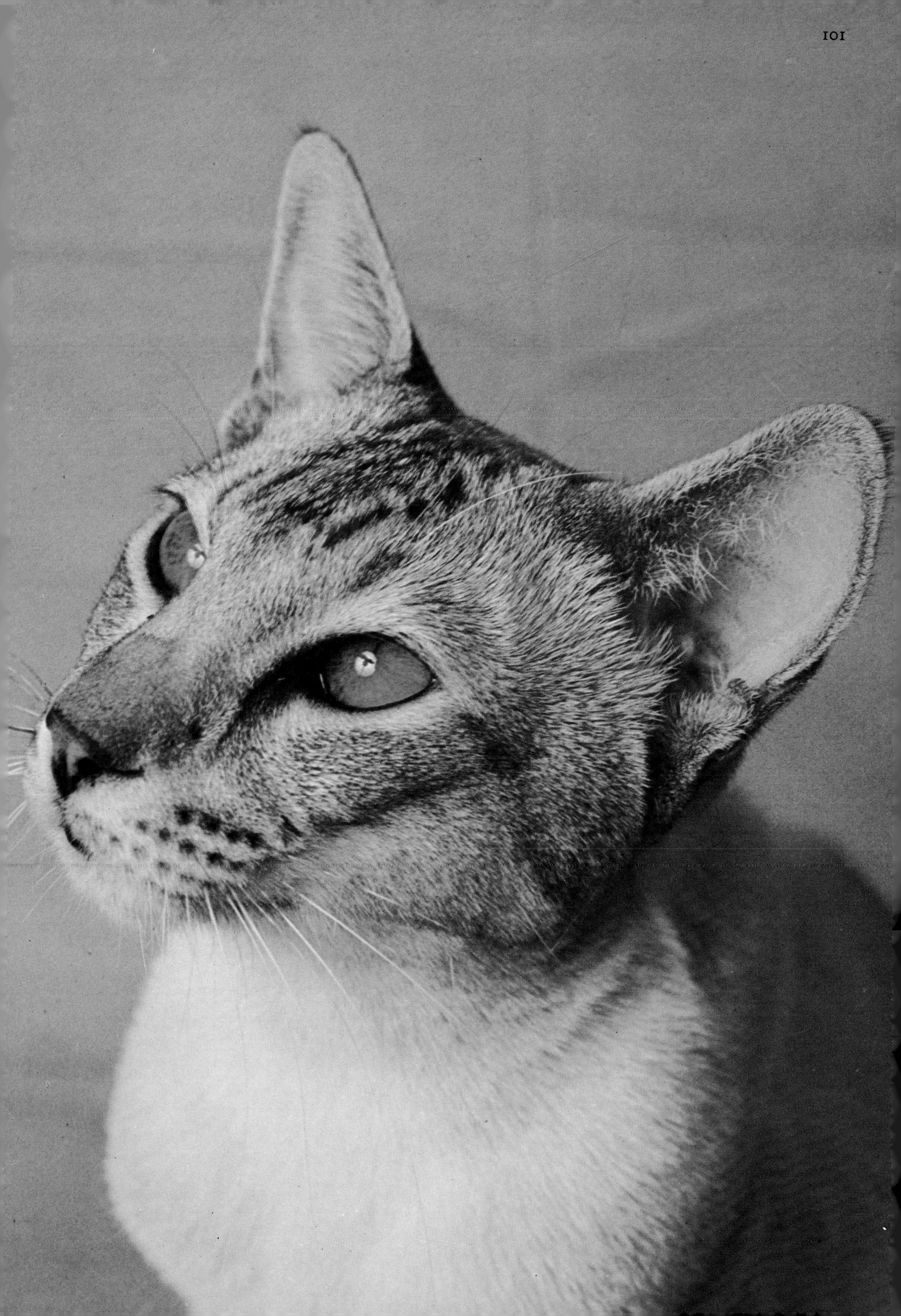

(b) *Chocolate Cream Point:* Ivory body; warm milk chocolate points uniformly mottled with cream. Nose leather is cinnamon but flesh or coral mottling is permitted with a blaze. Paw pads are cinnamon but flesh or coral mottling is permitted where the point color mottling extends into the pads.

(c) *Lilac Cream Point:* Glacial white body; frosty gray points with a pinkish tone uniformly mottled with pale cream. Nose leather is lavender pink although flesh or coral mottling is permitted with a blaze. Paw pads are lavender pink but flesh or coral mottling is permitted where the point color extends into the pads.

(d) *Seal Tortie Point:* Pale fawn to cream body, shading to a lighter color on chest and stomach; seal points uniformly mottled with red and cream. Nose leather is seal brown, and flesh or coral mottling is permitted with a blaze. Paw pads are seal brown, and flesh or coral mottling is permitted where the point color mottling extends into the pads.

Colors and Patterns
See pages 39–47

Copper
See Supilak

Cornish Rex

This unusual cat with its short curly coat originated from an accidental mutation in a litter of ordinary short-haired kittens produced by a farm cat in Cornwall, England in 1950. The breed was developed during the 1950s and achieved recognition in the United Kingdom in 1967.

The body of the Cornish Rex is Oriental – medium in length, slender, and strong – resembling that of the Siamese. Legs are long and straight with oval paws and the tail is long and tapering.

The head is medium in size, wedge-shaped, and narrowing to a strong chin. In profile the head is flat, with a sharp angle at the forehead and a straight line from forehead to nose. The large ears are set high and are wide at the base with rounded tips; eyes are medium and oval.

The coat is short and curly, and can be any color in Spectrum A and some

The Cornish Si-Rex is the result of the mating of a Cornish Rex and a Siamese.

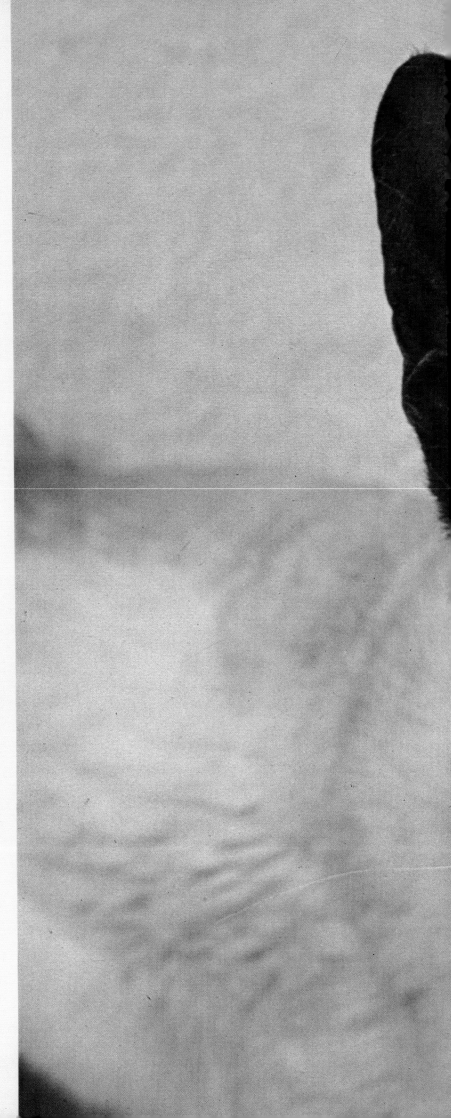

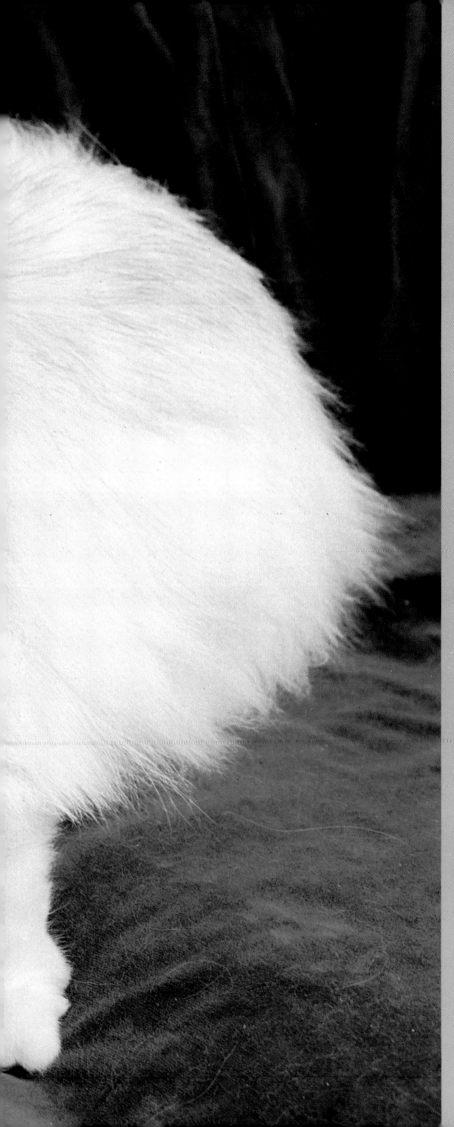

variations from Spectrum B (see Colors and Patterns). It is especially thick on the back and tail, giving the animal a plushy appearance. The curliness is due to the absence of guard hairs. Any white markings must be symmetrical except in the Calico. See also Rex.

Cougar
See Puma

Cream Abyssinian
See Abyssinian

Cream Burmese
See Burmese

Cream Persian

This popular variety originated from mating Blues and Reds.

The body should be solid and conform to Persian standards (see Persian). The tail should be short, but flowing.

The coat is long and dense, without white hairs, and should not be too red (see Colors and Patterns) or too harsh in texture. When the cat is molting the coat tends to darken, and regular brushing is required to maintain its cream color.

In mating, the occasional introduction of a Blue may help keep the pale cream color and avoid the 'hot' red tinge mentioned above. When a Cream is mated with a Blue male, the litter can contain Cream males and Blue Cream females. A Cream male mated with a Blue female may produce Blue male kittens and Blue Cream females. Female Creams are usually obtained by mating a Cream male with a Cream or Blue Cream female.

Left : Cream Persian or Long-hair.
Below : Cream Short-hair.

Cream Point
See Colorpoint Short-hair

Cream Short-hair

Cream Short-hairs are beautiful and much-admired cats, but are very difficult to breed to standard.

Body conformation should be that of the Short-hair (see American Short-hair and British Short-hair). Kittens are often born with barred markings which they may or may not lose as they mature; bars, stripes, and especially ringed tails are the most common faults in adult show animals.

Cream Tabby
See Colors and Patterns; Tabby

Cymric

The Cymric is a recognized breed and has been developed in America since 1960, but the CFA has not yet accepted it for show.

It is a hybrid, probably produced by mating a short-haired Manx with a Persian (though some consider it to be a mutation).

Except for its long coat, the Cymric should conform to the Manx standard (see Manx). Its most notable feature is its rounded rump, created by its short back, high hindquarters, and taillessness. The head is long and round with prominent cheeks; the nose is long; the ears are wide tapering to a point at the tip.

All colors and patterns of Spectrum A are possible (see Colors and Patterns).

Below : Cream Short-hair kitten.

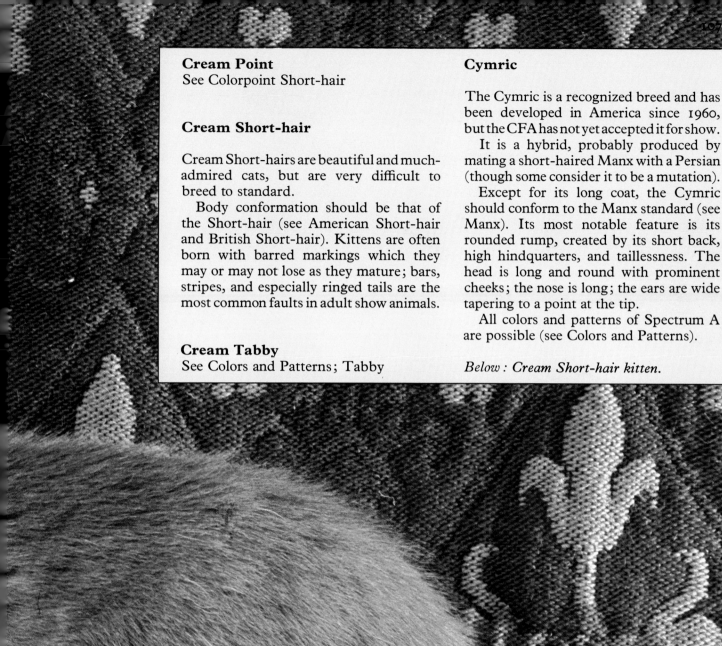

Desert Cat, Chinese
See Chinese Desert Cat

Desert Cat, Indian
See Indian Desert Cat

Devon Rex

The Devon Rex originated from a mutation in Devon, England in 1960, and at first was thought to be similar to the Cornish Rex. Subsequent events showed, however, that an entirely different gene was involved, and the Devon Rex was recognized as a separate breed in Britain in 1967. It has not yet been accepted by many American organizations.

Good-tempered and quiet, the Devon Rex makes an excellent pet for apartment dwellers.

The Devon Rex is of medium length with long slim legs, a wide chest and slender neck, and a long, thin, tapering tail.

The head is wedge-shaped with a flat skull, full cheeks, and a strong chin. There is a definite nose break. Whiskers and eyebrows are crinkled, and of medium length. Ears are large. The large eyes are oval and wide-set and should match the coat in color.

The coat is thinner than that of the Cornish Rex. It should be short, without guard hairs, fine, wavy, and soft. The Devon Rex is bred in most colors and patterns of Spectrum A and some of B (see Colors and Patterns). See also Rex.

Right : Devon Rex.
Overleaf : Two attractive Devon Rex kittens.
Overleaf, inset : An adult Devon Rex.

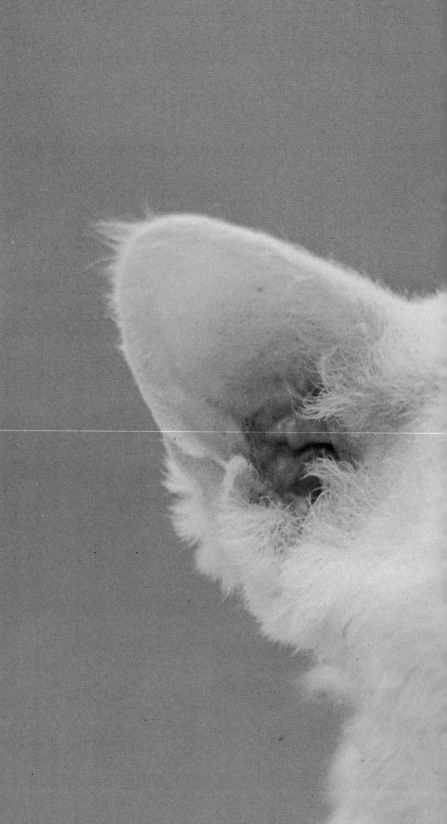

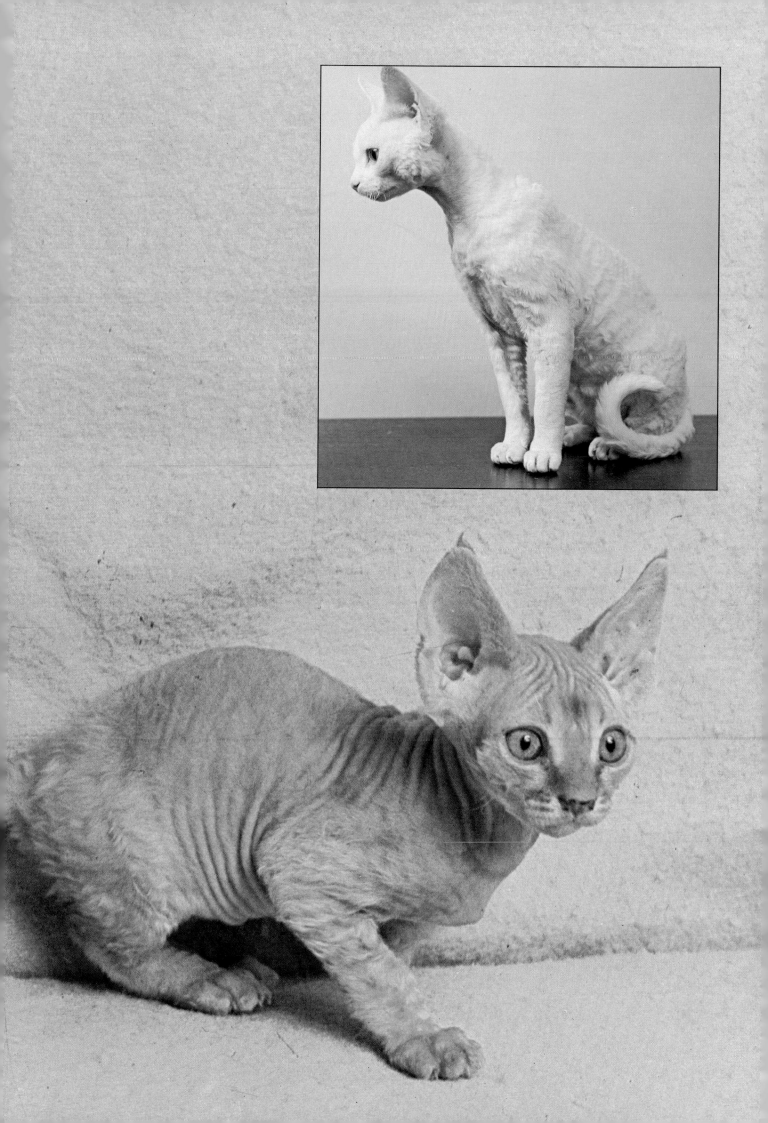

Dilute Calico
See Calico; Colors and Patterns

Egyptian Cat
See African Wild Cat

Egyptian Mau

Visitors to the ancient tombs at Thebes in Egypt can see a frieze showing a hunting scene in which a spotted cat is stalking ducks for an Egyptian hunter. Almost 3500 years later that cat's modern-day counterparts are living in many countries other than Egypt.

The Egyptian Mau – the only domesticated (natural breed) spotted cat – was developed during the 1950s from cats imported from Cairo, Egypt. It is still relatively rare, and has been only provisionally accepted for CFA shows.

The Mau's body should strike a nice balance between the compact Burmese and the lithe, elegant Siamese. It is graceful and medium in size and length with well-developed muscles. The hind legs are longer than the front legs; paws are small and almost round. The tail is medium in length, thick at the base and tapering slightly. Bodies that are too cobby or Oriental and tails that are short or 'whip' are considered faults.

The head is a modified, slightly rounded wedge without any flat planes. There is a slight rise from the bridge of the nose to the forehead which in turn flows into the arched neck without a break. The muzzle is rounded, and allowances are made for broad heads or stud jowls in males.

Ears are large, broad at the base, moderately pointed and alert. Hair on the ears should be short and close-lying, and the ears can be tufted. The inner ear is a delicate, translucent shell-pink.

The eyes should be neither round nor Oriental, but large, almond-shaped, and slightly slanted. All colors of Egyptian Mau have light, gooseberry-green eyes; a slight amber cast is permissible.

The coat of an Egyptian Mau should be medium but long enough for two bands of ticking separated by lighter bands of color to be visible. It is fine, silky, shiny, and resiliant.

There are some similarities between the Egyptian Mau and the Tabby pattern, and in fact in Britain the Mackerel Tabby pattern is allowed in show animals. The forehead carries the distinctive 'M' (or 'scarab') and frown marks which form lines between the ears. These lines run down the back of the neck, breaking into elongated 'spots' along the spine and coming together again at the rear haunches to become a dorsal stripe that continues to the tip of the tail.

Right and below : Egyptian Maus. These cats are still fairly rare and are not yet recognized in Great Britain. Below is a Bronze Egyptian Mau and on the right is a Silver.

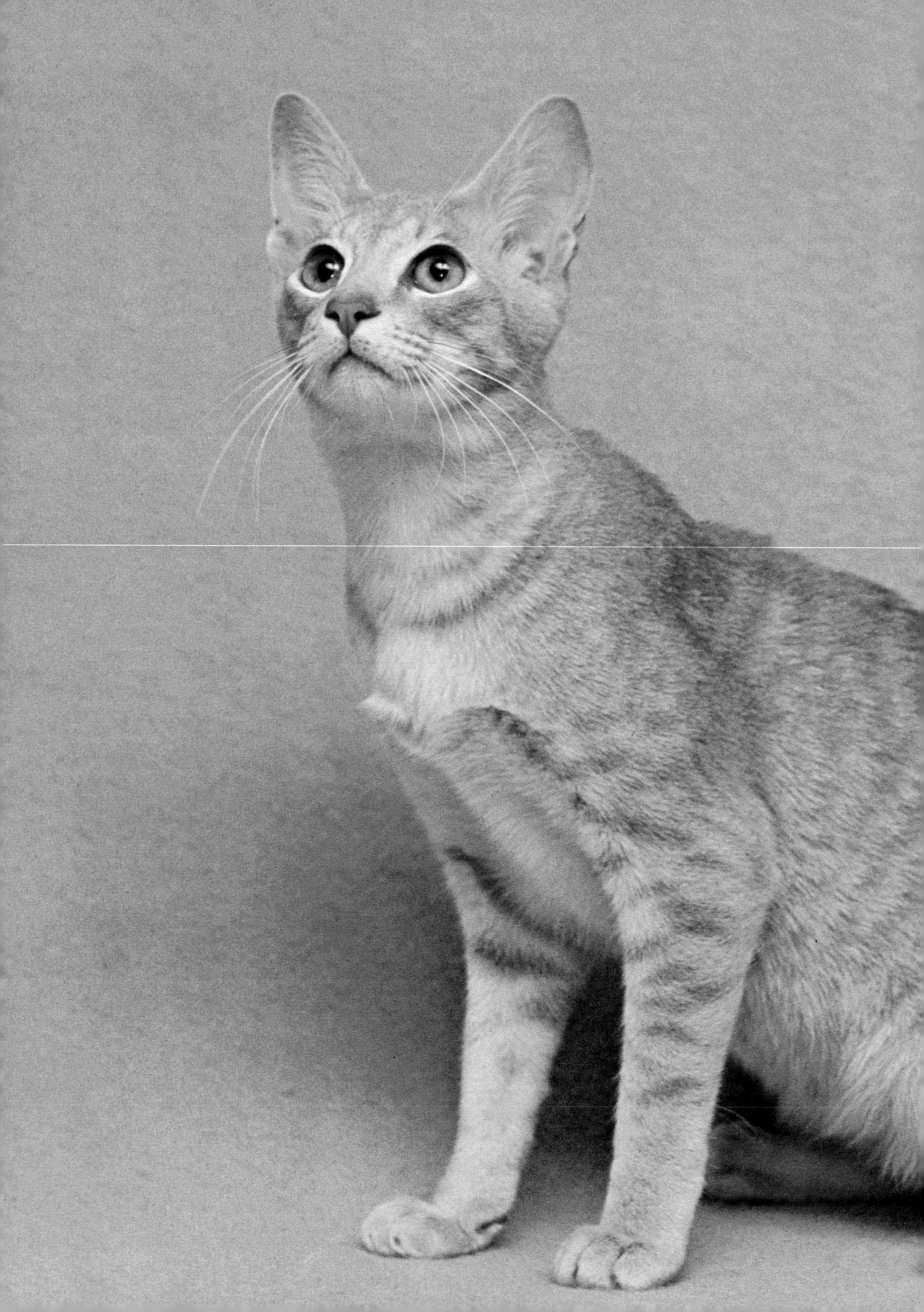

There are two 'mascara' lines on the cheeks. One starts at the corner of each eye and runs along the contour of the cheek; the other starts at the center of the cheek and curves up to almost meet the first.

The tail is heavily ringed (banded); there are one or more necklaces (preferably broken at the center) on the upper chest; and the upper forelegs are heavily barred. On the body random spots of varying size and shape should be evenly distributed, though the pattern need not be the same on both sides. The spots should be distinct, and may not run together to form a mackerel tabby pattern. There are 'vest pocket' spots on the underside of the body.

Transitional spots and stripes on the haunches and upper hind legs break into bars on the thighs and spots on the lower hind legs.

The Egyptian Mau is recognized in three colors: Bronze, Silver, and Smoke.

Bronze Mau
The ground color of the Bronze Mau's coat is light bronze becoming darkest over the shoulders and shading to tawny buff on the sides and creamy ivory on the underparts; markings are dark brown. Backs of the ears are tawny pink and tips are dark

Left : Egyptian Mau.

brown. Nose, lips, and eyes are outlined in dark brown; bridge of nose is ocher. The upper throat, chin, and the area around the nostrils should be creamy white. Nose leather is brick-red; paw pads are black or dark brown. There is black or dark brown hair between the toes and the same color extends slightly beyond the paws on the hind feet.

Silver Mau
The coat of the Silver Mau has a pale silver ground color with charcoal markings. Backs of the ears are grayish pink, and tips are black. The upper throat, chin, and area around the nostrils should be almost white. Nose leather is brick-red and paw pads are black. There is black hair between the toes, and black extends slightly beyond the paws on the hind feet.

Smoke Mau
The ground color of the Smoke Mau's coat is charcoal gray with a silver undercoat; markings are jet-black. Nose, lips, and eyes are outlined in black. The upper throat, chin, and the area around the nostrils should be the lightest charcoal gray color. Nose leather and paw pads are black. There is black hair between the toes, and black extends slightly beyond the paws on the hind feet.

European Wild Cat
Felis silvestris silvestris

The European Wild Cat ranges from Scotland and the more remote regions of Wales, throughout Europe (excluding Scandinavia) and into Western Asia. It is a protected species in Germany and recent surveys indicate that its population is increasing in Scotland.

These animals are virtually impossible to tame at any age, although some have been known to form loose, wary alliances with people. The European Wild Cat is a diurnal hunter, preying mainly on rabbits, rodents, and small birds. However young lambs, fawns, poultry, and beetles have been known to have been on the menu, and reports from the west coast of Scotland have it that some have also learned the art of fishing. The cats can be traced by their black droppings, which they do not cover up as domestic cats do, and by their paw prints which are usually in a straight line.

The European Wild Cat is about the size of a large domestic cat, but has longer leg bones and a shorter intestine. The skull and teeth are larger and the head is flat. The tail is of medium length and is very blunt; it is full, bushy, and is heavily ringed. The coat markings resemble the mackerel tabby pattern with black stripes on a gray ground. The underparts are buff.

Exotic Short-hair

The Exotic Short-hair was deliberately created by American breeders to fulfill a desire for a cat with the beauty of the Persian but without the problems associated with the Persian's long flowing coat.

The breed was produced through careful matings of American Short-hairs and Persians and is the only hybrid cross allowed today in the United States.

The Exotic Short-hair is identical to the Persian in conformation, with large round eyes, small ears, snub nose, cobby body, and short thick legs and tail (see also Persian).

The coat should be medium in length, dense, soft, and glossy. The Exotic Short-hair can occur in all the colors and patterns of Spectrum A (see Colors and Patterns).

Right : Scottish Wild Cat.

The European Wild Cat is not unlike a miniature Bobcat with a large fluffy tail.

Fishing Cat
Felis viverrina

The Fishing Cat gets its name from the fact that it inhabits low-lying, swampy, heavily forested areas that often occur near waterways in Asia, from India and Ceylon to Malaysia, Burma, and Taiwan.

It is a fearless, bold hunter that is not afraid of humans and has been known to attack goats, sheep, and calves. It has also been known to eat fish, but no one has ever reported actually seeing one fishing.

An adult Fishing Cat is about 2.5 feet long with a one-foot tail, and weighs, on average, 22 pounds. It is a thickly built cat with short, strong legs and slightly webbed toes. It has a short, coarse, tawny-gray coat with small dark spots on the body, dark streaks on the head and face, and narrow rings on the tail.

Flame Point
See Himalayan

Flat-Headed Cat
Felis planiceps

The Flat-Headed Cat is a very rare cat that is distributed throughout southern Asia – Borneo, Sumatra, and Malaysia.

It inhabits river banks and its diet includes fish, frogs, and small birds. It is a nocturnal hunter.

The Flat-Headed Cat is very small – only about 15–20 inches long with a six to eight inch tail, and weighs three to 4.5 pounds. It has a flat head with small, oval, widely spaced ears. The coat color is dark brown to deep rust, shading to white on the underparts. Some of the hairs may be white-tipped. The face is masked with white rings under the eyes, white whisker pads, and white lines that run from the corners of the eyes up over the forehead.

Above : A close-up of an Oriental or Foreign white Short-hair. (See also page 159.) Far right : Cinnamon Oriental or Foreign, an unusual type of Oriental Short-hair. Below : Geoffroy's Cat.

Foreign Black
See Oriental Black

Foreign Lilac
See Oriental Lavender

Foreign Short-hair

This term is used in the United Kingdom to refer to the conformation generally called 'Oriental' in the United States. Although Siamese come under this category, it generally is understood to cover Abyssinians, Burmese, Cornish and Devon Rex, Havanas, Korats, and Russian Blues, as well as the cats known in America as 'Oriental Short-hairs.' (See also Oriental Black, Oriental Lavender, Oriental Short-hair and Oriental White.)

Foreign White
See Oriental White

Frost Point
See Colors and Patterns; Siamese

Geoffroy's Cat
Felis Geoffroyi

Geoffroy's Cat is a South American native, found from Brazil to Patagonia and sometimes in parts of southern Bolivia.

It avoids areas inhabited by humans preferring mountainous regions and foothills. It is an excellent climber and, like the Jaguar, rests on the lower branches of trees and lies in wait for its prey. Its diet consists mainly of birds and small mammals, but it occasionally has been known to raid remote ranches.

The average size of this strongly built cat is two feet, with a one-foot tail. Its head is large in proportion to the rest of its body. The coat can be either gray or brown with dark spots. The ears are black with a brown patch.

*Above : Rex kitten.
Right : Known as
the Havana
Foreign or Chestnut
Brown Foreign in
the United
Kingdom the
Havana Brown
makes an
affectionate and
intelligent pet.*

German Rex

A cousin of the Cornish Rex, the German Rex was bred in Germany after the Second World War. During the 1950s it was used in developing the Rex breed in the United States.

Like the Cornish and Devon Rex, the coat is curly and without guard hairs.

See also Rex.

Golden Cat, Temminck's
See Temminck's Golden Cat

Hairless Cat
See Mexican Hairless; Sphynx

Havana Brown

The Havana Brown, an attractive, solid-color, mahogany-brown short-hair, was developed in England, where it is known as the Havana Foreign or Chestnut Brown Foreign. Solid brown short-hairs had occasionally appeared in cat shows for many years. The earliest example on record is a cat that was exhibited in 1894 as a 'Swiss Mountain Cat.' Again in 1930 a solid brown entry appeared in the category 'Brown Cat.'

After some years English breeders, working with Siamese, Russian Blues, and other short-hairs of mixed ancestry, were able to produce a solid brown short-hair that bred true (in other words, that produced solid brown kittens). Today the Havana Brown is an established breed, and only Havana-to-Havana matings are acceptable. The name derives from the rich, warm color, which is close to that of Havana cigars.

These affectionate, soft-voiced cats make admirable pets. They often have the unusual habit of using their paws to investigate strange objects by touch, instead of relying on their sense of smell as do most other breeds. They are generally healthy animals, but do suffer in very cold or damp weather.

Havana Brown kittens enjoy their evening meal.

The Havana's body is medium in length; firm and muscular with fine bones and graceful proportions. The legs are long and slim, with the hind legs slightly longer than the forelegs, and oval paws. The tail is also of medium length and should be in proportion to the body, with no sign of a kink.

The head is longer than it is wide with a distinct profile stop at the eyes, a fine rounded muzzle, and a definite break behind the whiskers. Ears are large and wide-set with slightly rounded tips; there is very little hair on either the outside or the inside. A Siamese head shape, a receding chin, and the lack of a profile stop at the eyes are all considered faults. Eyes are almond-shaped, slanting, and colored chartreuse green.

The coat is medium-length, smooth, and glossy; in color it is a rich, warm, chestnut or mahogany brown, as opposed to the shorter, darker, sable brown of the Burmese. The color must be even from nose to tail and from tip to root. White spots are considered faults. Whiskers should be brown; nose leather and paw pads are a rose color that harmonizes with the coat.

Havana Foreign
See Havana Brown

Himalayan

The Himalayan (called Colorpoint Long-hair in Britain) is the fastest growing breed in the world today. It is a magnificent hybrid that combines Persian conformation and coat quality with Siamese colors and patterns. In the comparatively short time since 1950, when the 25-year experimental breeding program first began to show results, the Himalayan has become the third most popular breed, surpassed only by the two breeds from which it was mainly developed – the Siamese and the Persian.

The enormous amount of genetic research in the United States, Britain, and Scandinavia to produce the Himalayan was necessary in large part because both the desired characteristics – long hair and colorpoint pattern – are carried by recessive genes (see the section on Genetics and Breeding, p. 236). In the United States breeders used Siamese and Persians, but in the United Kingdom experimenters used other short-hair colors as well, including the Havana Brown. In the United States today Persian-Siamese crosses can be registered as Himalayans, but in the near future only Persians will be permitted

for use in Himalayan hybridization.

The Himalayan should have a Persian-type conformation: large round head with small ears, large round eyes, and deep nose break; cobby body; short, thick neck and legs; and large round paws (see also Persian). Any similarity to either the Siamese or the Peke-Face Persian is considered a fault. All Himalayans have deep blue eyes.

The coat should be long, thick, and soft, with a full frill. The four classic colors and patterns of Spectrum B (Blue Point, Chocolate Point, Lilac Point, and Seal Point) are recognized. In addition, Hima-

Chocolate Point Himalayan.

layans are recognized in Blue Cream Point, Flame Point, and Tortie Point.

Other colors of Himalayans are also being produced, but have not yet been admitted to the show bench. The three most popular are the Lynx Point (see Colorpoint Short-hair), solid Chocolate, and solid Lilac (called Chocolate Self Long-hair and Lilac Self Long-hair in Britain).

The development of these varieties has led in turn to the production of other rare and exotic colors.

Blue Cream Point Himalayan
The body color of this breed is bluish or creamy white, shading to white on chest and stomach; points are blue with patches of cream. Nose leather and paw pads are slate-blue, pink, or both.

Flame Point Himalayan
The body color of this breed is creamy white, with orange flame points. Nose leather and paw pads are flesh or coral pink.

Tortie Point Himalayan
The body color of this breed is creamy white or pale fawn; points are seal brown with unbrindled patches of red and cream. A red or cream blaze on the face is desirable. Nose leather and paw pads are seal brown with flesh or coral mottling.

Himbur

The Himbur is a hybrid produced in America by crossing the Himalayan with the Burmese. The Himbur is recognized as a separate breed, but has not yet been accepted for show competition.

Indian Desert Cat
Felis ornata

The Indian Desert Cat is so closely related to the other wild cats that some zoologists maintain that it ought not to be classified as a separate species at all.

This small cat (about the size of the European Wild Cat) inhabits the drier regions of northwest India, feeding on the usual small rodents and birds.

Indian Lion
See Lion

Indian Tiger
See Tiger

Indo-Chinese Tiger
See Tiger

*Right: A pair of Indian or Asiatic lionesses in the Gir Forest, India.
Below: An Ocelot hunts for insects in a rotting tree trunk.
(See also page 154.)*

Jaguar
Panthera onca

Along with Pumas (Cougars or Mountain Lions) Jaguars are the only big cats left in the New World, and unfortunately their numbers are decreasing due to disturbance of their habitat and human exploitation for their skins. Distribution ranges from southern California through Central America into South America as far south as Patagonia.

The Jaguar prefers thick cover – jungle and swampland – but in California and at the southern edge of its range it will roam in plains and deserts in search of food. It has been found in mountainous regions in Colombia as well. An expert climber and a good swimmer, the Jaguar hunts mam-

mals such as deer and tapirs, wild turkeys, other birds, fish, and even small alligators and crocodiles. Jaguars have been known to attack cattle, but rarely humans.

Both the Jaguar and the Central American Jaguar (*Panthera onca centralis*) resemble the Leopard, with rosettes on a coat that varies from almost white to tawny. The rosettes, however, are larger than the Leopard's and therefore fewer in number; they become solid on legs and flanks, and form into rings near the end of the black-tipped tail. The average Jaguar is about 7.5 feet long (including a two-foot tail) and weighs about 250 pounds. Central American Jaguars are somewhat smaller.

A pair of Jaguars romp beside a desert waterhole in mid-summer.

Jaguarondi
Felis yagouaroundi

The Jaguarondi is a wild cat that ranges from southern Texas through Mexico to the Argentine.

A solitary animal that is as active by day as by night, the Jaguarondi lives on small mammals and reptiles, birds, and fish – and fruit, which is very unusual in a carnivorous animal. It is able to travel long distances by moving from tree to tree, and is also very fast on the ground.

Despite its name, the Jaguarondi bears no resemblance to the Jaguar, but has a head shaped amazingly like an otter's. Its long, graceful, short-legged body is either dark gray or brown (both colors can appear in the same litter). An adult is 4 to 4.5 feet long (including a 1.5-foot tail) and can weigh up to 20 pounds.

Japanese Bobtail

This is the indigenous cat of Japan, that originally came from China and Korea. It was imported into the US in 1969.

The Japanese Bobtail is a familiar figure in traditional Japanese art, and is believed to bring good luck; even today, Japanese Bobtails sit beside doorways or in shop windows with paws raised in greeting.

A slender but muscular, medium-sized cat, the Japanese Bobtail has hind legs that are longer than its forelegs. They are angled, however, so that the body is nearly level when the cat is standing. The legs are long and slender but strong.

The Japanese Bobtail's distinctive tail is usually about 4 inches long and can be straight or curved. The hair on the tail is longer and thicker than the rest of the coat, and looks like a pom-pom.

The head is an equilateral triangle, with high cheek bones and a broad muzzle that curves into a distinct whisker break. Ears are large and wide-set at right angles to the head. Eyes are also large, oval, and slanted.

The coat is medium in length, soft, and silky. Preference is given to the traditional good-luck color, *mi-ke* (mee'-kay): black and brilliant reddish-orange spots or shapes on a white ground. Other popular colors include black, white, red, black-and-white, red-and-white, tortoiseshell, and tortoiseshell-and-white; a variety of other colors is now accepted as well. Dramatic, contrasting colors are preferable. Colors of eyes, nose leather, and paw pads should harmonize with the coat as described in Spectrum A (see Colors and Patterns).

The solitary Jarguarondi, despite its name, is not at all like the Jaguar. It is able to move through the trees as quickly as it can on the ground and is one of the few carnivores which will pick and eat fruit from a tree.

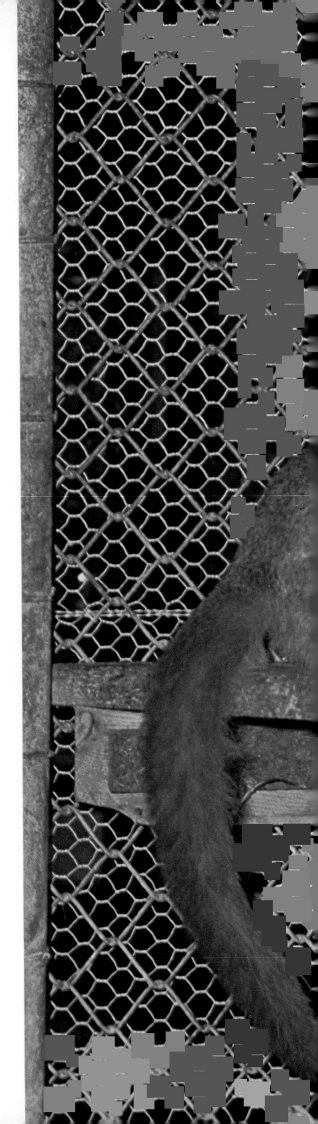

Javan Tiger
See Tiger

Jungle Cat
Felis chaus

The Jungle Cat, also known as the Swamp Cat, inhabits a large area from Egypt and the Middle East to Southeast Asia.

Jungle Cats like scrub and dry grassland, and often are found near small villages where they can obtain an occasional chicken to supplement their basic diet of other birds and small mammals. They have been tamed, but have never come to trust humans completely.

The Jungle Cat weighs about 20 pounds and is up to 3.5 feet long, making it slightly larger than a large domestic cat. The body is usually grayish brown with white underparts and chin. There are faint, broken stripes on the body and dark rings on the tail, which also has a dark tip.

Kaffir Cat
See African Wild Cat

Kodkod
Felis guigna

The Kodkod inhabits the foothills of the Andes in South America. It is becoming very rare and has not been studied in detail.

Kodkods live mainly on rodents and other small mammals, and occasionally raid farmyards for chickens. They may hunt in packs.

This small cat is only 1.5 feet long with another nine inches of tail. The coat is grayish brown with small black spots on the back and sides. Black lines run up the face and over the head, and the tail is ringed in black.

Korat

The Korat, the good-luck cat of Thailand, has a long and well-documented history, dating from a Thai manuscript that may have been written as early as 1350 AD. Korats come from the northeastern province of the same name, and are called *Si-Sawat* in Thailand (a reference to a fruit plant whose seed is the same silver blue color as the Korat).

The breed was exhibited in Britain as early as 1896 and a few were brought to the United States during the 1930s, but there were no serious attempts at breeding until the late 1950s. The Korat Cat Fanciers' Association was founded in 1965 to protect the purity of Korat bloodlines and ensure that only those cats with Thai ancestry are registered.

Korats are rare even in Thailand, and have been highly valued there for many years; originally they could not be purchased, but had to be given as a gift. They are quiet, intelligent cats who take an active part in family life. They dislike sudden noises, however, and are apt to be nervous at shows.

The Korat is a hard, muscular, medium-sized cat that is surprizingly heavy for its size. Its lines are all curves; it has a rounded back, well-proportioned legs (the hind legs are slightly longer than the front), and a medium-length tail that tapers to a rounded tip. A *non-visible* kink is permitted in show animals.

The head is heart-shaped, from the eyebrow ridges to the strong, well-developed chin. There is a slight stop between the nose and the forehead, and the nose curves slightly downward just before the nose leather. Ears are very large, with rounded tips and a wide flare at the base. Eyes are also large; they are rounded when fully open but have an Oriental slant when partly or completely closed. Eyes should be a luminous green but an amber cast is acceptable. (The green color usually appears in mature cats; kittens often have yellow, amber, or golden-green eyes.)

The coat is close-lying and is silver blue in color tipped with silver. The tipping appears all over the coat especially where the hairs are shortest. The coat should be free of shading, tabby markings, and white spots. Nose leather and lips are dark blue or lavender. Paw pads range from dark blue to lavender with a pinkish tinge.

Far left: The Jungle or Swamp cat roams throughout the Middle East and Southeast Asia. Below: A color portrait of the Oriental Lavender, discussed in detail on page 157.

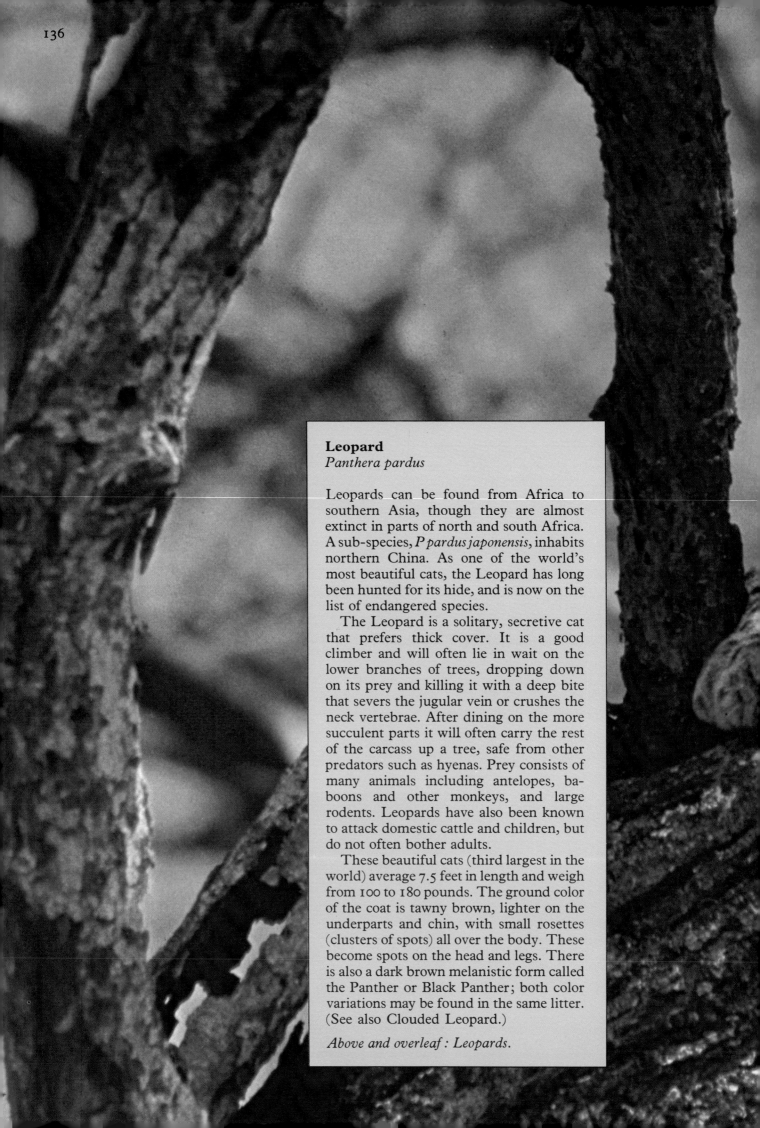

Leopard
Panthera pardus

Leopards can be found from Africa to southern Asia, though they are almost extinct in parts of north and south Africa. A sub-species, *P pardus japonensis*, inhabits northern China. As one of the world's most beautiful cats, the Leopard has long been hunted for its hide, and is now on the list of endangered species.

The Leopard is a solitary, secretive cat that prefers thick cover. It is a good climber and will often lie in wait on the lower branches of trees, dropping down on its prey and killing it with a deep bite that severs the jugular vein or crushes the neck vertebrae. After dining on the more succulent parts it will often carry the rest of the carcass up a tree, safe from other predators such as hyenas. Prey consists of many animals including antelopes, baboons and other monkeys, and large rodents. Leopards have also been known to attack domestic cattle and children, but do not often bother adults.

These beautiful cats (third largest in the world) average 7.5 feet in length and weigh from 100 to 180 pounds. The ground color of the coat is tawny brown, lighter on the underparts and chin, with small rosettes (clusters of spots) all over the body. These become spots on the head and legs. There is also a dark brown melanistic form called the Panther or Black Panther; both color variations may be found in the same litter. (See also Clouded Leopard.)

Above and overleaf: Leopards.

Leopard Cat
Felis bengalensis

The Leopard Cat is the most common small wild cat in Southeast Asia; it is also found in Tibet and northern India, China, and eastern Siberia.

Hunted both for its hide and for exploitation as an exotic pet, the Leopard Cat faces extinction if measures to preserve it are not taken soon. Its popularity as a pet is hard to fathom, since it is as ferocious and hard to tame as the European Wild Cat – and as unhappy in captivity.

It lives in hilly areas and on the outskirts of jungles, but avoids the denser forests. It is a good climber and often drops on its prey like a leopard; its diet includes large birds, small mammals, and even the occasional small deer. Leopard Cats are nocturnal hunters.

The Leopard Cat is only about 2.5 feet long, and looks something like a small leopard. Its coat is yellowish or grayish, with dark brown spots (not rosettes). The spots on the tail form into bands at the tip. Streaks extend from the forehead down the back of the head, and from the corners of the eyes, under the ears and down the neck. Ears are black with a white spot.

Leopard, Clouded
See Clouded Leopard

Leopard, Snow
See Snow Leopard

Lilac Burmese
See Burmese

Lilac Cream Point
See Colorpoint Short-hair

Lilac Lynx Point
See Colorpoint Short-hair

Lilac Point
See Colors and Patterns; Siamese; Himalayan

Lilac Self Long-hair
See Himalayan

Lilac Tortie Burmese
See Burmese

Far left: A Leopard Cat kitten. Below: An adult Leopard Cat perched on a tree. Leopard Cats are slightly larger than the European Wild Cat (page 116) but are equally difficult to tame.

Lion
Panthera leo

Lions once ranged from Europe and the Middle East throughout Africa and India. Man has sadly decimated the Lion population however, and today the 'King of Beasts' survives in only a few small areas in Africa and in the Gir Forest in India.

One reason Lions are such easy victims is that they prefer open country. Their diet includes both large animals (antelopes, zebras, and goats) and small animals (rats), and they also eat carrion. Lions are the only social cats, living in prides of up to thirty comprised of an older male, several females and adolescent males, and as many as ten cubs. Lions usually hunt by executing a carefully planned campaign; a small party will chase a herd of herbivores into an ambush formed by the rest of the party. Females often make the kill; cubs do not join the hunt until they are two.

Both African and Indian males average about 9 feet in length and weigh from 300 to 400 pounds; females are smaller and lighter. The body is long and muscular, with short powerful legs and a thin, medium-length, tufted tail. Some experts claim that the Indian Lion is slightly stockier than the African. The head is long with a straight profile and small, very rounded ears. The African male has very thick hair on its mane (which covers the head and shoulders), elbows, and tail. The Indian sub-species has a smaller mane, but more hair on chest, elbows, and tail. Females do not have manes.

Cubs are born with spots which all but disappear as they mature. Coat color of the adult varies from pale fawn to tawny blue, and the mane is tawny brown to black.

Below : A pride of Lions rests on the Serengeti Plains.

Lions occasionally find peace by climbing trees.

Lion, Mountain
See Puma

Little Spotted Cat
See Tiger Cat

Long-hair
See Persian

Lynx, Bay
See Bobcat

Lynx, Caracal
See Caracal Lynx

Lynx, Northern
See Northern Lynx

Lynx Point
See Colorpoint Short-hair

Magpie
See Bi-colored Persian; Colors and Patterns

Maine Coon

Maine Coon Cats, according to New England experts, are the biggest, smartest, most beautiful cats in the world. Its name comes from an early legend that these king-size (thirty pounds) cats are part raccoon.

Although this is obviously impossible, the Maine Coon's actual origins are as obscure as those of the American Short-hair. Some experts believe that it is the result of uncontrolled matings between the short-haired cats brought to America in the seventeenth century and Angoras or Persians imported by sailors in the 1800s.

Justifiably proud cat lovers in Maine have kept pedigree information on Maine Coon Cats for many years; the Maine Coon Cat Club was established in 1953, and every year since then a Maine State Champion Coon Cat has been selected in Skowhegan, Maine.

The body of a Maine Coon is large, muscular, broad-chested, and long, so that it has a rectangular shape. Legs should be medium in length, in good proportion to the body, and substantial. Paws are large, round, and well-tufted; the tufts make it easy for the cat to 'snowshoe' across the frozen Maine countryside in winter. The tail is long and tapering.

The head is medium, with a square muzzle, high cheekbones, firm chin, and a medium-length nose. The ears, which are set high and well apart, are large, tapered, and tufted; 'Lynxline tips' (tufts on the tips of the ears) are especially desirable. Eyes are large and wide-set, slanting slightly upwards toward the ears.

Maine Coon Cats are penalized if they have a delicate bone structure, and are disqualified for having a receding chin, crossed eyes, a kinked tail, or an incorrect number of toes.

The coat is heavy and shaggy, shorter on the shoulders than on the stomach and haunches. The shagginess is most noticeable on the underparts and on the long-haired tail. There is a 'muttonchops' frill on the chest. Texture of the coat is silky and smooth. An even coat is a fault.

The Maine Coon Cat is bred and recognized in every color of Spectrum A (See Colors and Patterns); in addition, any color or combination of colors except those in Spectrum B is accepted. Eyes may be green, gold, or copper; in whites, eyes may also be blue or odd-eyed.

Maltese

The Maltese, which was very popular in America at the turn of the century, is no longer a recognized breed. It is a short-haired Blue that has now been superceded by the Russian Blue.

Manchurian Tiger
See Tiger

Manx

There are many myths about the tailless Manx: one, for example, tells how the Manx was very late for the Ark and had its tail cut off by an over-anxious Noah as he slammed the door shut. Attempts have also been made to establish a relationship between the Manx and the bobtailed cats of the Orient.

In fact, the taillessness of this unique breed undoubtedly arose from a mutation within the small confines of the Isle of Man – a 221-square-mile island in the Irish Sea off the west coast of England. Recent research has shown that the Manx has a different phenotype and is not genetically related to the Far Eastern cats.

The Manx makes a delightful pet – healthy, intelligent, and fond of people.

Left: Tabby patterned Manx Cat.
Overleaf: A white Manx cat.

It is also reputed to be an excellent ratter. Breeding Manx cats can be tricky, however. The mutation which causes the taillessness affects the vertebral column; if vertebrae are missing anywhere other than at the end, kittens will be born dead. Thus breeding is best left to experts.

There are three variations found in Manx cats. *Rumpies* have no tail at all, and a hollow is found where the tail usually begins. Only Rumpies are accepted for show. *Stumpies* have one- to five-inch tails, and *Full-tails* or *Longies* have complete tails. All three tail lengths are often found in the same litter.

Over all, the Manx should give the impression of roundness. The body should be solid, compact, and well-balanced, with a round, broad chest, substantial round short front legs, and a round rump ('as round as an orange,' to quote the British Standard) created in part by the short back and high hindquarters.

The hind legs are much longer than the forelegs, with a heavy, muscular thigh and a strong lower leg. In America Manx cats are disqualified for having a visible tail joint, polydactylism (wrong number of toes), or the inability to stand or walk properly (the high, deep flanks can cause a rabbit-like gait).

The head is round, with prominent full cheeks and a rounded muzzle. Ears are wide-based, tapering, and rather long, but should be in proportion to the head.

The beautiful, plush coat is something like a rabbit's, with a short, thick, cottony undercoat and harder, glossier guard hairs.

The Manx is recognized in all the colors and patterns of Spectrum A (see Colors and Patterns), and in combination of colors and patterns which includes white. Eyes, nose leather, and paw pads should correspond with the coat color.

There is considerable variation in the number of points allocated to the Manx characteristics in the United States and Britain as is shown in the following chart.

	USA	Britain-Europe
Taillessness	10	15
Hindquarters (height)	–	15
Body	25	–
Back (shortness)	5	15
Rump (roundness)	–	10
Legs/Feet	15	–
Flank (depth)	5	10
Coat (not color)	15	10
Head Ears	10	10
Color Pattern	5	5
Eyes	5	5
Condition	5	5

Manxamese

The Manxamese is a short-haired hybrid obtained by crossing Manx with Siamese to produce a cat with the colorpoint pattern of Spectrum B (see Colors and Patterns).

Marbled Cat
Felis marmorata

The Marbled Cat is another beautiful, but extremely fierce wild cat about which very little is known.

It is found on the slopes of the Himalayas, throughout Burma and the Malay Peninsula, to Borneo and Sumatra. It hunts along riverbanks and in small clearings, and is known to be a good climber. Thus it is reasonable to assume that fish and birds form some part of its diet, along with small rodents and other mammals.

The Marbled Cat is only a little larger than a domestic cat, and very much resembles the Clouded Leopard. It has a soft, heavy coat with body markings that are large on the back, gradually decreasing into spots on the legs and head, and forming rings on the tail. Lines on the head run from the eyes to the ears. The muzzle of the Marbled Cat is finer, its ears longer, and its tail longer and thicker than those of the Clouded Leopard.

Margay Cat
Felis weidi

The Margay Cat inhabits Central and South America. Not much is known about its habits, but it is reported to spend a lot of time in trees. Like the Ocelot it is in

Below: The Margay Cat.

demand as an 'exotic pet,' but since even kittens raised in captivity can be unpredictable and dangerous when they mature, most zoologists discourage the practice. (See also Ocelot, page 154.)

The Margay is closely related to the Ocelot and is similar in appearance. It averages three feet in length, including a one-foot tail, and weighs about 12–15 pounds. Ground color ranges from tawny to gray with clearly defined black spots that often have a center corresponding to the ground color. There are horizontal lines on the neck and chest, spots on the paws, and rings on the tail. Underparts are usually white with a yellowish tinge, and there is a white streak on either side of the nose and under the eyes. The ears are longer than the Ocelot's and are dark-rimmed on the inside.

Mau
See Egyptian Mau

Mexican Hairless

This is an extinct breed; the last known pair, said to have been purchased from Indians who claimed they were the last of an Aztec breed known only in New Mexico, died early in this century.

They are said to have had very short fur on their backs and tails which fell off in warm weather. They had long bodies, long thin tails, and wedge-shaped heads with big ears, long whiskers, and amber eyes. Both cats were flesh-colored with a mousey gray shade along the back.

Moon Cat
See Sphynx

Mountain Cat
Felis jacobita

Little is known about the Mountain Cat (sometimes called the Andean Cat). It lives in the mountainous regions of Chile, Peru, Argentina, and Bolivia, and its diet consists mainly of small rodents.

Though small (less than 2.5 feet total length) it is strongly built. Its coat is light brown with darker brown bars. The tail is about a foot long, very bushy, and has a dark brown tip.

Mountain Lion
See Puma

Northern Lynx
Felis lynx

The Northern Lynx once roamed throughout the temperate forests of the Northern Hemisphere but civilization – the disappearance of much of its habitat and exploitation for its long, soft fur – has driven it into remote regions where dwindling numbers of the animals are still persistently hunted.

Most of the Northern Lynx population is found today in Alaska, where it is still relatively common. Other small pockets exist in northern New England, the Adirondacks, and the Great Lakes region of North America and in parts of Scandinavia, the Balkans, and the Iberian Peninsula.

The Northern Lynx inhabits thick bush and forest doing most of its hunting at night. It is an agile climber and a good hunter; its diet is varied, including birds, rodents, and other small mammals such as foxes, roe deer and skunks.

Bigger and more beautiful than a Bobcat, the average Northern Lynx is just under four feet long and weighs between 36 and 40 pounds. Its long soft fur can be almost white, but usually it is a mixture of tawny and yellow hairs with some longer silvery guard hairs and a few indistinct spots, giving it a shadowy, etherial appearance. A ruff of long hair on the cheeks outlines the face. The ears are long and light brown in color with a long slender black tuft; the tail has a black tip.

Far right: A close-up of the face and head of an Egyptian Mau (page 112). Below: Northern Lynx.

Ocelot
Felis pardalis

Paradoxically the Ocelot is in grave danger of extinction on one hand, because of the high commercial value of its beautifully marked coat, while on the other hand, it is becoming increasingly popular as an 'exotic' pet. Unfortunately it is very difficult to breed ocelots in captivity.

It inhabits dense, tropical areas from Central America to Equador and Northern Argentina. It could once have been found in southwestern United States, where it is now nearly extinct.

Ocelots spend much of their time relaxing in trees, but hunt on the ground, often in pairs. They generally remain in their own clearly defined territory. Their diet includes almost any animal they can overpower – deer, fawns, domestic lambs and calves, rodents, frogs, monkeys, birds, and even snakes. Since they are good swimmers, fish may be included as well.

Many experts believe that the Ocelot has two breeding seasons (June and December). Litters usually consist of two kittens, born in a nest of grass or other soft material built in a hollow log or under a bush.

The average male Ocelot is four feet long (including a one-foot tail) and weighs about 35 pounds. Females are somewhat smaller. It has a small head and rounded ears, a long neck, a relatively short body, and long thick legs.

The coat varies from pale grayish yellow to cinnamon; the ground color is darkest on the back gradually becoming lighter on the sides. The underparts, chin, and whisker pads are a creamy white. Markings consist of dark brown spots and blotches, bordered in black. The blotches on the tail tend to be darker and more solid. Two stripes run from either side of the nose up over the forehead, two more cross the cheeks, and there are four or five stripes on the neck.

The Ocelot (or Margay) as a Pet :
Ocelots and margays are the most popular wild cats now being kept as pets. Both are reasonably docile, but do require a lot more patience, knowledge, dedication, and work than ordinary house cats. Before you acquire an ocelot then, you will have to be sure that you have the time, energy, and facilities necessary for the success of the enterprise. Check too to see if there are any local ordinances in your community which prohibit keeping a wild animal as a pet.

Right : A young Ocelot.

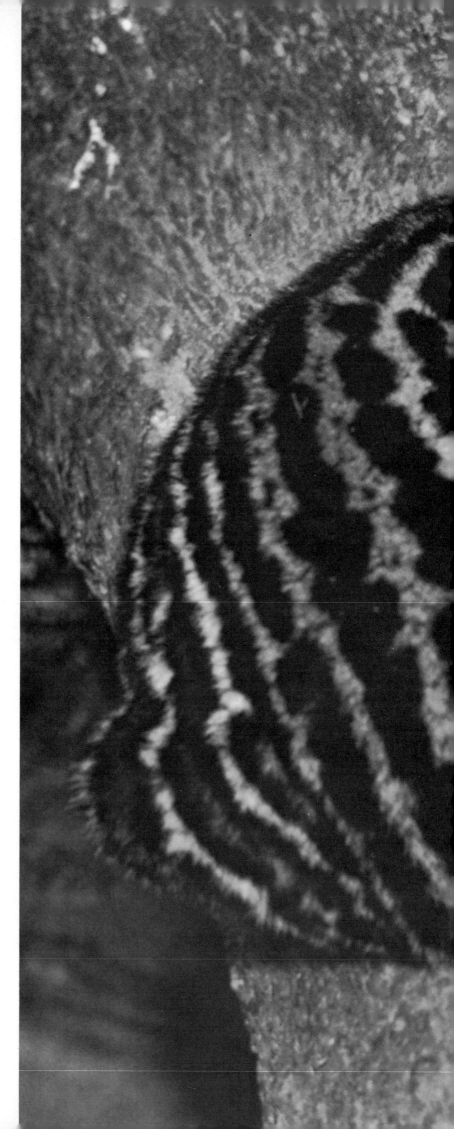

Decide if you want an ocelot or a margay. Ocelots are much larger, and therefore margays are usually considered more suitable for homes with children. Ocelots love water and will be especially happy if there is a swimming pool – though they will also enjoy playing in the bathtub or under the garden hose. Decide too whether you want a male or a female. Males are usually more docile and survive surgery (neutering) better than females.

If you cannot find an older pet that someone wishes to part with, you will have to order one from an importer. Be sure to check the organization's reputation carefully. Be prepared to spend a lot of money and wait some time for delivery. You may also have to spend some time nursing the animal back to health; many arrive at their new homes with nutritional deficiencies and parasites.

Both ocelots and margays are very playful. The ocelot loves to leap at you from ambush and wrap itself around your legs. The margay prefers to jump down on you from heights. Teaching them to play games ('fetch' for example) can often provide an acceptable substitute.

Ocicat

The Ocicat is a hybrid breed produced in America by mating a Siamese Chocolate Point male and an Abyssinian-Siamese crossbred female. It is now produced by

crossing the Abyssinian with the American Short-hair, or either of these with the Ocicat itself. Although it is a recognized breed, it has not yet been accepted for championship competition.

The Ocicat has an Oriental conformation, with a head like the Abyssinian and golden oval eyes. The coat pattern is spots on a pale cream ground color, with tabby markings on the throat, legs, and tail. The markings are dark chestnut brown for the Dark Chestnut Ocicat or milk chocolate color for the Light Chestnut. The fur is short and silky.

Odd-eyed White
See White Persian; White Short-hair

Orange-eyed White
See White Persian; White Short-hair

Oriental Black
See Oriental Short-hair

Oriental Lavender

The Oriental Lavender (called Foreign Lilac in Britain) is only produced when both parents carry genes for Blue and Chocolate. The coat should be frost-gray with a pinkish tone; eyes should be a rich green (see also Oriental Short-hair).

Below: Oriental Short-hair kittens.

Oriental Short-hair

The Oriental Short-hair is a hybrid produced by crossing Siamese, American Short-hairs, Colorpoint Short-hairs, and other Oriental Short-hairs. It has the conformation of the Siamese (called 'Foreign' in Britain), but the colorpoint pattern has been eliminated. It has provisional acceptance from the American CFA.

Just as many breeders spent years trying to transfer the colorpoint pattern to Persian-type cats (see Himalayan), others are working to transfer the more exotic colors and patterns of Spectrum A (see Colors and Patterns) to the Siamese-type.

There are only a few minor differences between the Oriental Short-hair and Siamese standards. Males may be a bit larger than females; the tail is thin at the base; and cats are penalized for having crossed eyes. Oriental Short-hairs may have green or amber eyes in addition to bright blue (see also Siamese).

Oriental Short-hairs are recognized in White, Ebony (black), Blue, Chestnut (Self-Chocolate), Lavender (Lilac), Red, Cream, Silver, Cameo, Ebony (or Black) Smoke, Blue Smoke, Chestnut (or Chocolate) Smoke, Lavender Smoke, and Cameo (Red) Smoke and in Classic, Mackerel, and Spotted Tabby patterns.

Oriental White

Oriental Whites can be difficult, delicate cats, very prone to diseases.

The Oriental White should have a completely white coat with no trace of a colorpoint pattern. Eyes can be green or bright blue; gold-eyed cats are not accepted for the show bench. Paw pads and nose leather are pink.

Ounce
See Snow Leopard

Below : Oriental Short-hair.

Pallas's Cat
Felis mamul

Pallas's Cat inhabits wooded and mountainous areas in Asia from Persia to Tibet and Mongolia; it is also found in the deserts of China. Its diet consists mainly of rodents and other small mammals.

This unusual looking animal is about the size and weight of a domestic cat. It has an exceptionally low forehead and low, wide-set ears. Some experts argue that these features enable the cat to hunt by sight instead of by sound, crouching behind large rocks and watching its prey unobserved.

Two coat colors have been reported: dark orange and silvery gray. The face markings include black stripes on the sides, black and white rings around the eyes, and spots on the forehead. There is a 'beard' of long fur around the cheeks. The tail is very bushy, with dark rings and a black tip.

Pampas Cat
Felis colocolo

The Pampas Cat is another wild cat about which very little is known. Once it could be found throughout the swamps and grasslands of Argentina and Uruguay, but today it has become very rare, facing extinction as its habitat is swallowed up by civilization.

It does most of its hunting at night; its prey consists primarily of birds and small mammals.

The Pampas Cat has silvery gray fur that becomes lighter on the sides and light gray on the underparts. It has a dark, reddish brown line down its back. Other, lighter lines run across the back and sides and from the eyes to the ears.

Panther
See Leopard

*Right: Pallas's Cat.
Below: Oriental
Lavender.*

Panther, Black
See Leopard

Above: Peke-Face Persian.
Left: White Persian.

Parti-colored Persian
See Bi-colored Persian; Calico; Persian;
Tortoiseshell Persian; Colors and Patterns

Peke-Face Persian

The Peke-Face Persian was developed in
the United States during the 1930s from
Standard Red and Red Tabby Persians. It
is not recognized in England.

As the name suggests, the face should
bear as close a resemblance as possible to
that of the Pekinese dog, with a very short
depressed nose, high forehead, large round
eyes, and prominent ears. Peke-Face
Persians often have deformed teeth and
lower jaws, leading to difficulties in
breathing.

In all other respects, conformation
should be that of the Persian (see Persian).

Peke-Face Persians are only recognized
in two colors: Red and Red Tabby (see
Colors and Patterns).

164

Persian

The Persian is the aristocrat of domestic cats – the paragon of pedigreed breeds. The origin of the breed is obscure, but many experts believe that it first appeared in Persia and Turkey, and is a descendant of some Asian wild cat. During the nineteenth century, long-haired cats were known to exist in Afghanistan, Burma, China, Russia, and Turkey.

Persians are usually sedate, dignified cats, very conscious of their beauty and their position in life. Their coats must be groomed daily to keep them free of loose hair, knots, tangles, and grease – and to keep the rugs and furniture relatively hairless. Show cats are usually groomed twice a day.

The Persian is a medium to large cat, but quality is more important than size. It has a cobby body: low-lying, long, and thick-set with a deep chest, massive shoulders and rump, and a short, well-rounded middle. The back is level and the legs short, thick, round and firm. Like all pedigree cats, the Persian has five toes on its front paws and four on its hind paws; polydactylism (an incorrect number of toes) is a fault. The tail is short and bushy, and should be in good proportion to the body. It is carried at an angle lower than the body, without curves.

The head, set on a short, thick neck, is round and massive, with full cheeks, powerful jaws, and a well-developed chin. The ears, which are small, wide-set, and tilted slightly forward, have long tufts of hair. The eyes are large, round, and set far apart. The nose is broad and short – almost snubby – and there should be a definite stop, or break, in the profile.

The Persian coat should be thick and soft, fine textured, with a glossy lively appearance. It should be long all over, including the shoulders; the ruff (longer hair around the head) should be immense, and continue down in a deep frill between the front legs. The condition and coloring of the coat is more important than body type. Persians are recognized in every color and pattern of Spectrum A (see Colors and Patterns), and Persian-type cats are also recognized in the colorpoint pattern of Spectrum B (see Himalayan).

Persian Tiger
See Tiger

Platinum Burmese
See Burmese

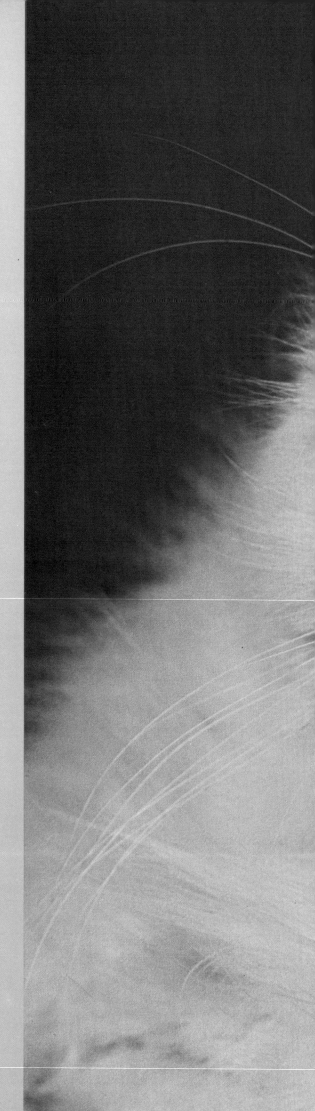

White Persian (or White Long-hair).

166

Platinum Tortie Burmese
See Burmese

Puma
Felis concolor

The Puma, also known as the Cougar and the Mountain Lion, originally ranged throughout the deserts, forests, jungles, and mountains of the Americas. The destruction of its habitat and relentless hunting have, however, considerably reduced its range.

Pumas are strong, athletic animals, capable of jumping about fifteen feet in the air, covering more than 35 feet in one forward leap, and dropping over fifty feet to the ground. Males will travel up to fifty miles when hunting. The average life span is about eighteen years.

Pumas breed all year round, producing litters of between one and four cubs. Kittens remain with their mother for up to two years, but adult Pumas are solitary animals. They are avid hunters and will eat almost anything from mice to domestic cattle. Pumas rarely attack humans.

There are about thirty sub-species, which vary greatly. The smaller Pumas of the tropics can have a total length of only four feet and weigh as little as 46 pounds, while the larger cats living in cooler climates may measure up to eight feet in

length and weigh up to 260 pounds. Generally, females are smaller and more slender. In appearance the Puma rather resembles the lioness but its head is rounder.

Coat color can vary from light fawn to dark brown or black, but short reddish brown fur with white underparts is most common. Body markings consist of a black ridge running down the back to the end of the black-tipped tail. Whisker pads are black, and black lines run from the pads up the sides of the nose to the eyes. Kittens are born with spots and rings on the tail which disappear as they mature.

Below : Puma.

Ragdolls

Ragdolls are a unique breed that derive their name from their limpness; when picked up they relax completely and flop over like a ragdoll. They are very placid creatures and completely fearless. This is, in fact, their weakness, for it puts them in great danger of injury, especially from other animals and children. They should never be allowed to wander or make contact with other animals, and require a great amount of care and attention.

Ragdolls are similar to Birmans, but are larger and have thicker fur. Markings are either Seal Point or Lilac Point with the Birmans' white boots and mittens.

Red Abyssinian
See Abyssinian

Red Burmese
See Burmese

Red Lynx Point
See Colorpoint Short-hair

Red Persian
See Solid Red

Red Point
See Colorpoint Short-hair; Himalayan

Red Self
See Colors and Patterns; Solid Red

Red Tabby
See Colors and Patterns; Tabby

Solid Red (US) or Red Self (UK).

Rex

The Rex is a spontaneous mutation of the domestic cat. Its short, tightly curled coat gives it an exotic appearance that appeals to many. Moreover, many people who are allergic to cat hairs find the Rex, because of its special coat, the perfect pet.

The first Rex was discovered in 1950 on a farm in Bodmin Moor, Cornwall, England; his mother was a short-hair with a normal coat and his father unknown. He was named Kallibunker. His owner, Mrs Nina Ennismore, contacted professional breeders and a program to preserve the mutation was established. Kallibunker was first bred back to his dam, resulting in several curly-coated kittens. A careful combination of inbreeding and outcross ing to normal-coated cats established the Kallibunker bloodline (see Cornish Rex).

The second spontaneous Rex mutation was discovered in Germany by Dr Scheur-Karpin. This Rex was a female named Lammchen, and her breeding was also carefully planned to preserve the bloodline (see also German Rex).

The next important mutation was Kirklee, a kitten discovered in Devon, England in 1960. Genetic research resulted in the discovery that a different gene was involved in this mutation: Cat Gene 1 was therefore assigned to the Kallibunker (Cornish Rex) bloodline and Cat Gene 2 to the Kirklee bloodline (see also Devon Rex).

A long-haired version of the Rex was found in an animal shelter in San Bernadino, California a few years later. This variety was named the Marcel. This cat was successfully used in several short-coated Rex breeding programs, but there was not much interest in preserving the long-haired variety and it has since died out.

The Rex's arched back and muscular hind legs make it capable of attaining very high speeds as well as helping it make quick starts, changes of direction and high jumps. Its overall conformation is discussed in more detail in the entries for Cornish Rex and Devon Rex.

The coat, which is very important, is short, very soft and silky, and tightly curled due to the complete absence of guard hairs. This unique coat makes the Rex very warm to the touch.

Show cats are disqualified for having a kinked or abnormal tail, an incorrect number of toes, or any coarse guard hairs.

Most Rex colors are those described in Spectrum A (see Colors and Patterns), but Other Rex Colors (ORC) are also accepted for show.

Rex.

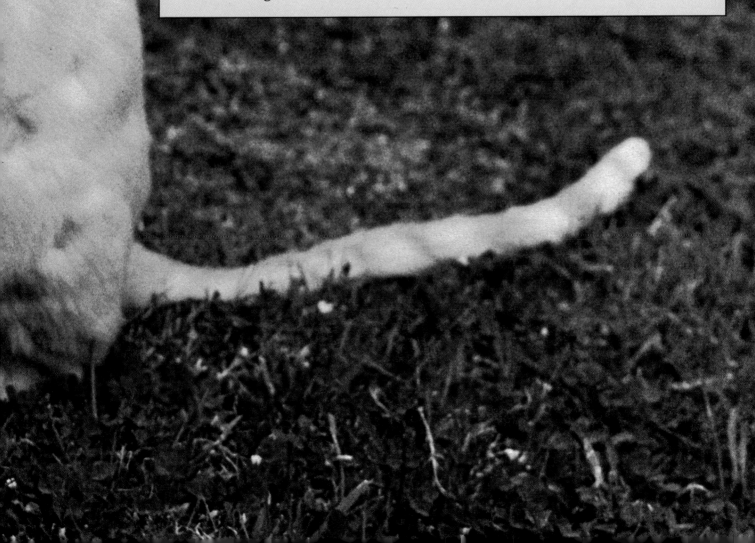

Ruddy Abyssinian
See Abyssinian

Rumpie
See Manx

Russian Blue

The origin of the Russian Blue is not known. It is thought that sailors brought the breed from Archangel, Russia to England, and in fact, it was called the Archangel Cat for many years. It is said to have also been the treasured pet of the czars.

Besides being beautiful, Russian Blues are quiet, shy, gentle animals that become firmly attached to their owners. They make lovely pets, especially in smaller houses or apartments.

The Russian Blue has fine bones and a long, lithe, sinuous body. Legs are long and the tail tapering. The neck is long and slender, though it appears short because of the thick fur on the neck and the animal's very high shoulder blades (ideally, the shoulder blades should almost touch behind the neck).

The head, which is short, should be wedge-shaped with a narrow, flat skull and a straight, receding forehead.

Below and inset : Russian Blue.

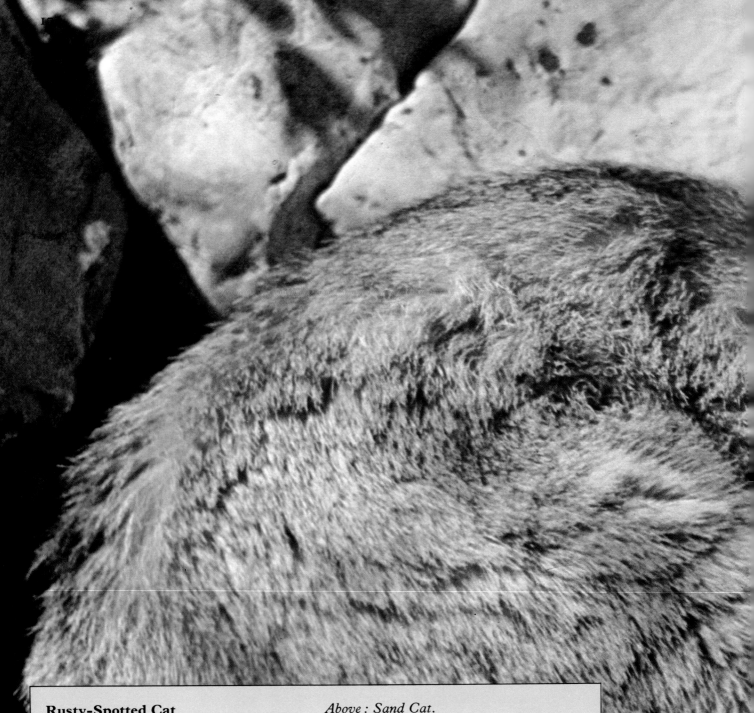

Rusty-Spotted Cat
Felis rubiginosa

The Rusty-Spotted Cat is a small, elegant, wild cat that inhabits tall grass and brush areas in southern India and Sri Lanka. Although it is not hunted it is extremely rare. Its diet includes small birds and mammals.

Unlike most other wild cats, Rusty-Spotted kittens are quite easily tamed.

The average Rusty-Spotted Cat weighs just over three pounds and is about two feet long (including a nine-inch tail). Coat color varies from reddish brown to fawn, with white underparts. The spotted markings, which tend to be elongated, are very pronounced on the back, fade on the sides and become darker and more dense on the legs. There are only a few faint markings on the tail, but the tip is almost black. There are streaks on the forehead and

Above : Sand Cat.

from the corners of the eyes to just under the ears, similar to the Leopard Cat.

Sable Burmese
See Burmese

Sand Cat
Felis margarita

The Sand Cat inhabits semi-desert areas and rocky wastes in North Africa and parts of the Middle East as far north as southern Russia.

Very little is known of its life and habits, but it is thought to be a nocturnal hunter preying chiefly on rabbits and small rodents. It is also reported to dig shallow burrows in the sand where it hides during

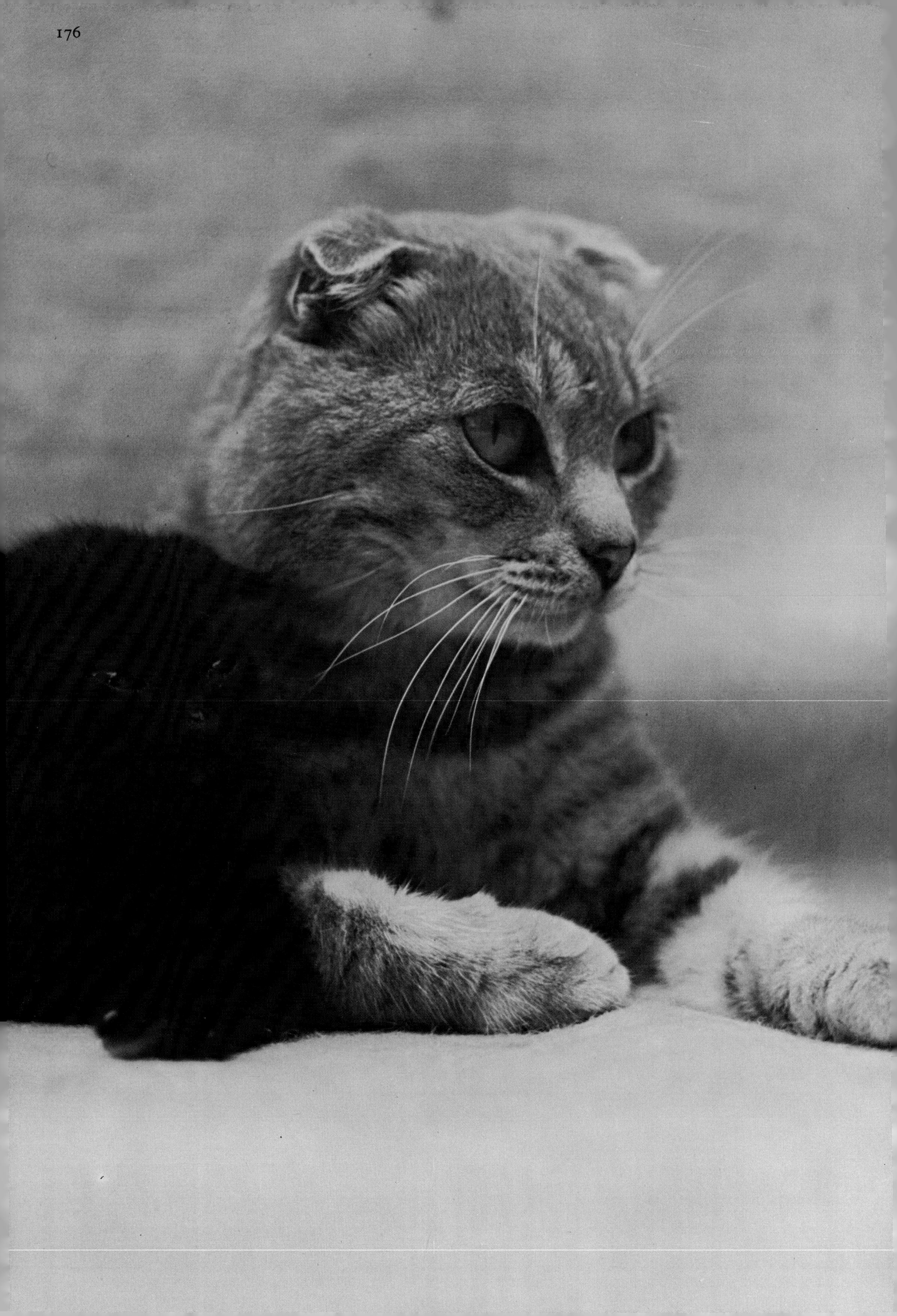

Left and above : Scottish Fold.

the daytime and where it bears its young.

The Sand Cat is about the size of a domestic cat with a very short muzzle and large, expressive eyes. Its ears are set far apart – almost at the sides of the head; they are wide at the base with a black patch on the back. The paws are heavily furred, which is probably a great help in the sandy areas where the animal lives.

Coat color varies from yellowish to grayish brown. The only markings are a few stripes on the legs and tail which also has a black tip.

Scottish Fold

Mutations of cats with dropped ears have undoubtedly appeared at intervals throughout history, but the Scottish Fold, first discovered on a farm in Perthshire, Scotland in 1961, represents the first attempt to preserve the mutation.

It is a very appealing cat that is growing in popularity, but is also meeting with some opposition; it is recognized as a breed but is not accepted for show competition.

The Scottish Fold has a round, short, muscular body with a short, thick coat. The head is large with large round eyes and the ears have a distinctive fold.

Scottish Wild Cat
See European Wild Cat

Seal Lynx Point
See Colorpoint Short-hair

Seal Point
See Colors and Patterns

Seal Tortie Point
See Colorpoint Short-hair

Serval
Felis serval

Servals range across Africa south of the Sahara inhabiting open savannahs and never straying far from a water supply.

They are nocturnal hunters that prey on mole rats and other rodents and small mammals, lizards, and birds. Since they are good climbers as well as strong swimmers, Servals have been known to capture nesting birds. Litters usually consist of three kittens; the female Serval population is much larger than the male.

A distinctive, strikingly beautiful cat, the average Serval is about twenty inches high and measures about three feet in length with a very short (nine- to ten-inch) tail. It is a light, slender animal that weighs less than twenty pounds. The legs are long and powerful; the head is comparatively small with large, slightly rounded ears that are set high and very close together.

The smooth, short coat is reddish yellow (although a black form has been reported), with underparts that are almost white. Markings are a mixture of spots and stripes. Black stripes run from the forehead, down the neck, and over the shoulders. There are large black spots on the back and flanks, becoming smaller on the lower sides and legs and very small on paws and cheeks. A row of spots runs up from the sides of the nose to the forehead. The tail is ringed and ends in a black tip. Ears are black on the outside with a distinct white spot in the middle.

A Serval spits at the cameraman.

Shaded Cameo
See Cameo; Colors and Patterns

Shaded Silver Long-hair

Still recognized as Shaded Silver Persian in North America and other parts of the world, this breed was dropped in Britain in 1902 because of the difficulties involved in differentiating between darker-than-average Chinchillas and lighter-than-average Shaded Silvers. See also Colors and Patterns.

Shaded Silver Persian
See Colors and Patterns; Shaded Silver Long-hair

Shadow Point
See Colorpoint Short-hair (Lynx Point)

Shell Cameo
See Cameo; Colors and Patterns

Short-hair
See American Short-hair; British Short-hair

Left: Shaded Silver Persian.

Siamese

The Siamese, most popular of all the breeds, almost certainly originated in Siam (Thailand). Legend has it that they were bred by the Kings of Siam and used as palace guards, pacing the walls and leaping on the backs of intruders. This story is speculative to say the least, but we do know that pictures of Seal Points were published in Siam some 400 years ago.

In 1885 the first Siamese cat was exhibited at Crystal Palace in London. It was one of a pair that had been presented to the then British Consul-General in Bangkok, Owen Gould. Siamese cats appeared in America around 1890 and were first exhibited in the early 1900s; the first Standard was published in Britain in 1892.

The original standard called for a stocky, round-headed cat that was often sickly, cross-eyed, and kinked-tailed – quite different from the sleek, elegant animal seen on today's show bench. The revised standard was issued in 1902 and was an immediate success.

Much of the Siamese's popularity lies in its personality. They are intelligent, playful, individualistic animals, prone to demanding a lot of attention and becoming very jealous if it is not forthcoming. They show much more open affection than other breeds and take easily to a lead. Most have a harsh, often imitative voice; the queen's call when she is in heat can be loud, penetrating, and very disturbing.

Siamese have large litters (often as many as five kittens). Kittens are born white, with the points developing as the fur grows. Both females and males mature at a very early age, and care must be taken if females are to be kept from mating before they are really ready for childbearing.

Siamese have been used in producing a surprising number of modern breeds including the Balinese, Bombay, Colorpoint Short-hair, Havana Brown, Himalayan, Lilac Foreign Short-hair, Manxamese, Oriental Short-hair, and Tonkinese.

Today's Siamese is a medium-sized cat with a long, slender, but muscular body and long slender legs. The body must be neither flabby nor bony; the tail is long, thin, and tapering; the paws oval and rather small.

The head should be a long, tapering wedge, medium-sized and in good proportion to the body. It narrows in straight lines to the muzzle and strong chin; there should be no whisker break. Allowances are made for jowls, however, in stud cats. The skull is flat; in profile there is a long

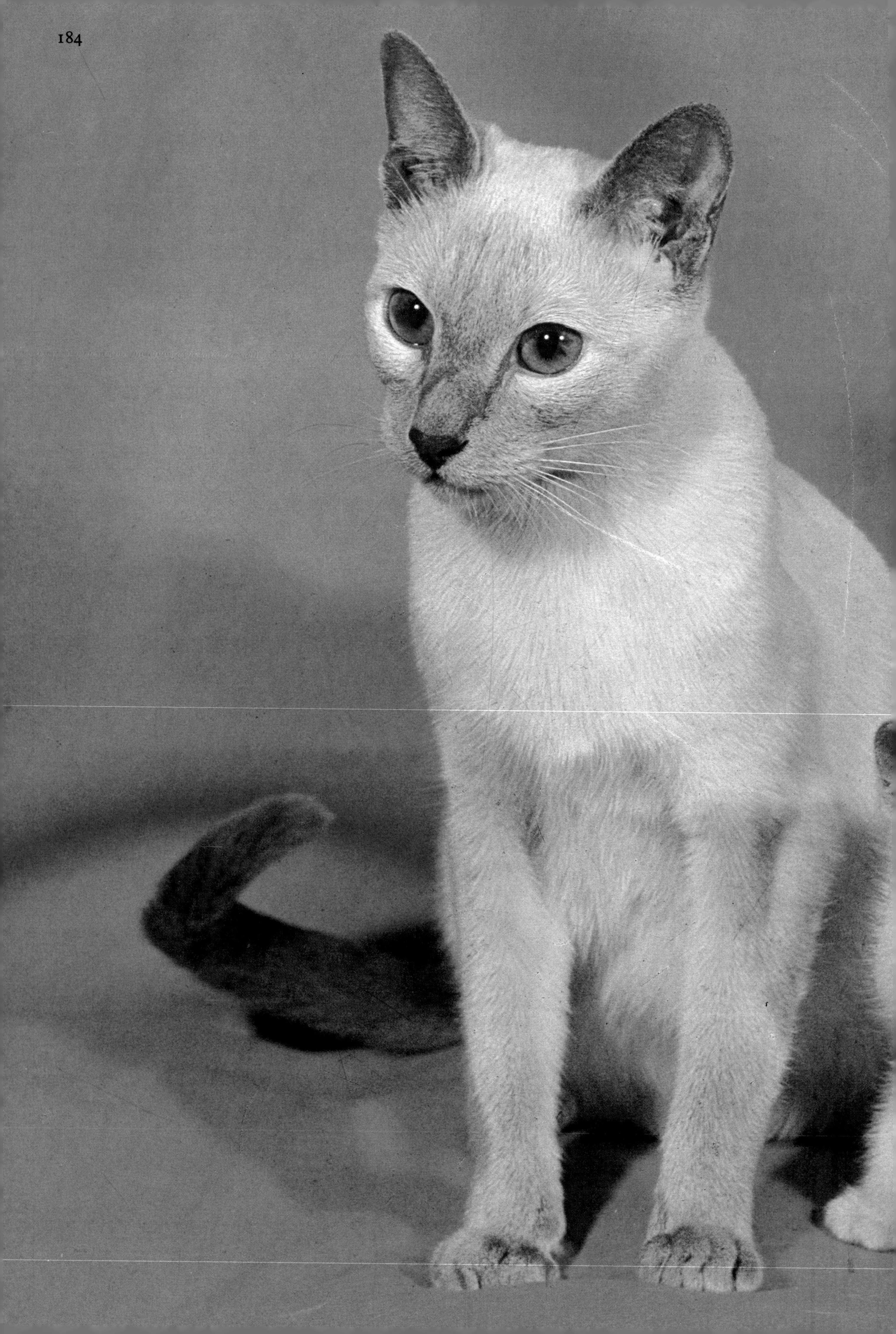

straight line from the top of the head to the top of the nose.

The ears continue the lines of the wedge. They are very large, wide at the base, pointed, and pricked. Eyes are medium sized and almond-shaped, slanting toward the nose in lines that correspond with the shape of the wedge. Show cats cannot have crossed eyes.

Other grounds for disqualification in show cats besides crossed eyes are: any evidence of ill-health; weak hind legs; mouth breathing due to nasal obstruction or a malformed jaw; emaciation; a visible tail kink (though a slight kink is acceptable in Britain), white toes and/or feet; and eyes that are any color but blue. Cats are penalized for having off-color or spotted paw pads or nose leather.

The coat is short, sleek, and close-lying. Siamese are recognized in the colorpoint pattern described in Colors and Patterns, but some notes of general interest about the various colors are appended below.

Blue Point Siamese

The Blue Point was the second variety of Siamese to gain recognition. There are early reports of its being seriously bred in England and America by the 1920s. The Blue Point is possibly more gentle than the other varieties, and loves to be hand-groomed. When grooming, take care not to brush too hard or too much; this will not only leave brush marks in the fur, but will also take out the undercoat.

Chocolate Point Siamese

The Chocolate Point is one of the earliest known varieties, but was only recognized in 1950. This was because the continual occurrence of blue in the points produced a much colder tone, leading people to believe that they were just Seal Points with poor coloration. The development of the colorpoints usually takes longer for Chocolate Point kittens than for other varieties, and the coat tends to grow far darker with age. Chocolate Point coats also react more to climatic conditions, making them difficult to breed and maintain in good condition.

Lilac (or Frost) Point Siamese

Lilac (or Frost) Points were first bred in America from parents who carried recessive genes for Blue and Chocolate. Coloration standards vary between Britain and America (see Colors and Patterns).

Preceding page : Seal Point Siamese.
Left : Lilac Point Siamese and her kitten.

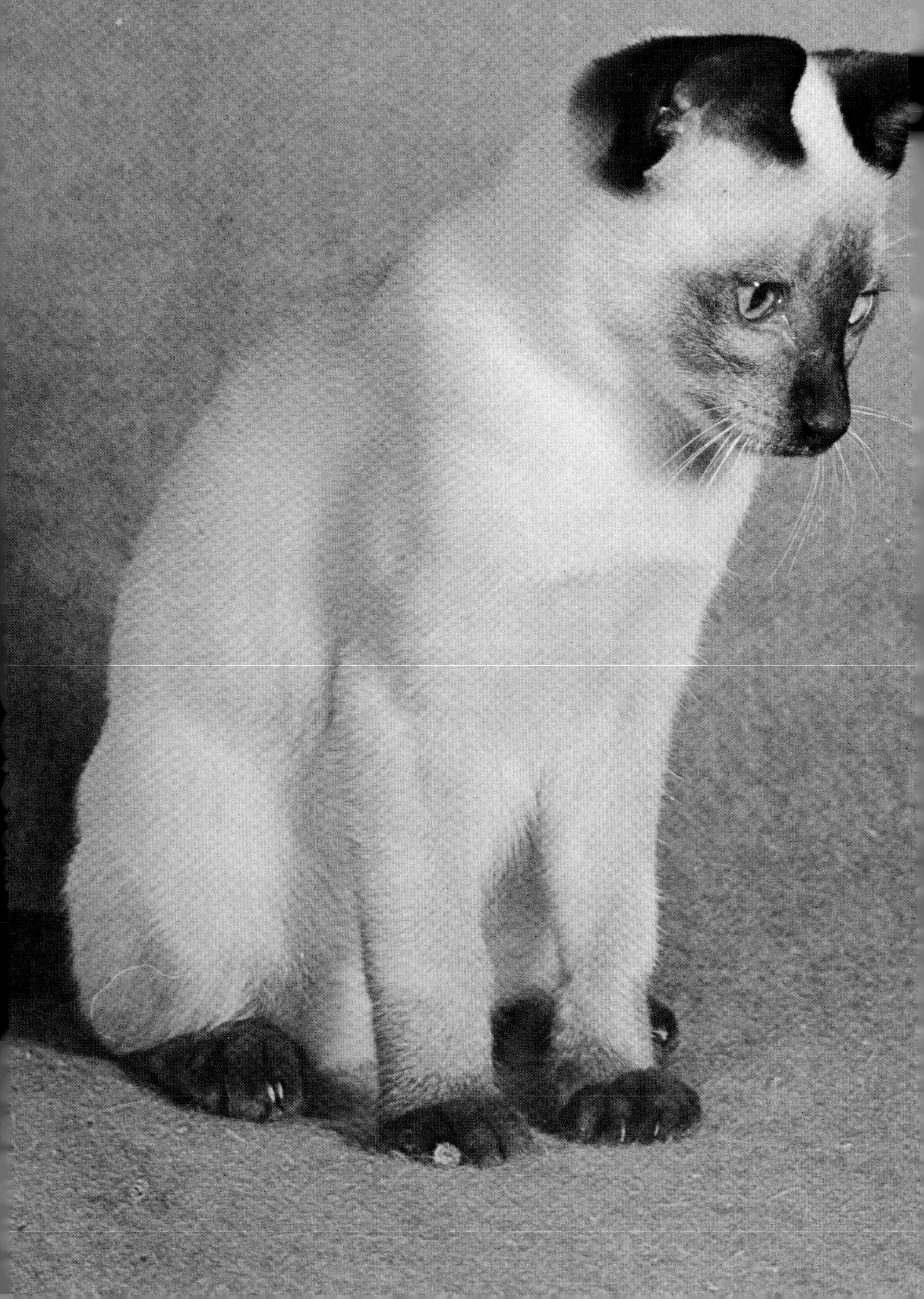

Seal Point Siamese
The Seal Point was the first Siamese variety to be recognized, and is still the most popular. The points begin to form on kittens as a smudge around the nose which becomes more definite as they grow; the line between mask and ears is not clearly defined until the cat is fully adult. The coat darkens with age on most cats and points are apt to develop brindling.

Siberian Tiger
See Tiger

Silver Mau
See Egyptian Mau

Silver Persian
See Chinchilla

Silver Point Siamese
See Colorpoint Short-hair

Silver Tabby
See Colors and Patterns; Tabby Persian; Tabby Short-hair

Left : A four-month old Seal Point Siamese kitten.
Below : Smoke Persian (or Long-hair).

Si-Rex
See Cornish Rex; Devon Rex; Rex

Si-Sawat
See Korat

Smoke Cameo
See Cameo; Colors and Patterns

Smoke Long-hair
See Smoke Persian

Smoke Mau
See Egyptian Mau

Smoke Persian

The Smoke Persian (in Britain, the Smoke Long-hair) is probably the result of uncontrolled matings between White, Black, and Blue Persians around the turn of the century.

The dense, silky coat requires frequent grooming to remove loose hairs and keep it looking its best; the coat should be brushed away from the body.

Most Smoke Persians today are produced by mating Smoke to Smoke, though the type is sometimes improved by outcrossing to a Black. Kittens are born black.

188

Conformation should be that of the Persian (see Persian); patterning is described in Colors and Patterns.

Blue Smoke Persians
These cats are recognized as a separate variety and result from mating Smoke and Blue Persians.

Smoke Short-hair

Black Smoke and Blue Smoke Short-hairs are recognized in the United States, but not in Britain; several European countries have provisional standards. The fur is short and white with black or blue tipping (see also Colors and Patterns). Conformation should be that of the American Short-hair.

Snow Leopard
Panthera uncia

The Snow Leopard, also known as the Ounce, is one of the five big roaring cats (the others are the Jaguar, Leopard, Lion, and Tiger). It is extremely rare – there are probably only about 400 left – as its beautiful thick coat makes it a prime target for hunters. Both the United States and United Kingdom have banned the import of skins, but the remedy may have come too late.

Snow Leopards range through mountainous regions of southern Russia, Afghanistan, Tibet, Mongolia, and western China. They generally spend the summer in the rocky grasslands between the tree line and the snow line (12,000–18,000 feet) moving down into the upper valleys for the winter. Prey consists of sheep, deer, wild goats, smaller mammals, and birds, depending on the habitat.

Cubs are born in the spring in litters of two to four and remain with their mother until the following spring.

The Snow Leopard is similar in size and weight to the Leopard: about two feet high at the shoulders, averaging 4.5 feet long with another three feet of tail, and weighing from 100 to 200 pounds. It has a long, luxuriant, pale gray coat, with yellowish shading and white underparts. There are black rosettes which are like the Leopard's but bigger; as on the Leopard they shrink to spots on the legs and head. The small ears are outlined in black with a small white spot in the middle. The long, bushy tail is also marked with rosettes which turn into rings near the tip which is black.

Solid Red

The Solid Red, also known as the Red Self or Red Persian, is rare because reproducing the coat color is very difficult; it is often more orange than deep red. Eliminating tabby markings, especially on the face, is also a major problem.

Somali

Somalis are long-haired Abyssinians that are rapidly becoming popular in America. They are slightly larger than short-haired Abyssinians and can be either red or ruddy. The coat is dense and requires comparatively little grooming; there should be a full ruff, with shorter hair on the shoulders. Somalis are quiet, affectionate cats with alert dispositions.

Above: Smoke Persian.
Right: An exceptionally rare photograph of an exceptionally rare animal – the Snow Leopard or Ounce is bordering on extinction as its beautiful coat has made it a prime target for the hunter's gun. The most optimistic estimates put its numbers at 500.

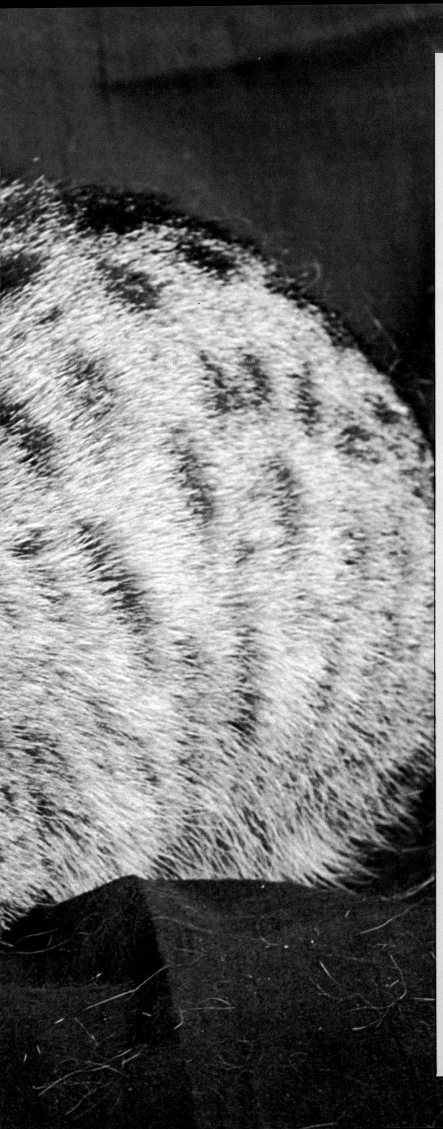

Sphynx

The Sphynx, also known as the Canadian Hairless, *Chat Sans Poils* (cat without hair) and Moon Cat, closely resembles the now-extinct Mexican Hairless.

This mutation was first recorded in 1966, born to a domestic Black and White in Ontario, Canada. The breed was developed from this specimen.

The Sphynx looks something like a sad, wrinkled Pug dog, and is very warm and smooth to the touch. Although they have been produced in the United States and Britain as well as in Canada, there does not appear to be much interest in the breed. It has been recognized by a few associations, but is not generally accepted for show competition.

The body of the Sphynx is slender, with good muscles and a longish tail. The head is a rounded wedge shape with a short nose; ears are very wide at the base and slightly rounded at the tip; the eyes are golden and slightly slanted. The cat has no whiskers.

It may be any color, but solid colors must be even and parti-colors symmetrical. The face, ears, paws, and feet are covered with a fine short down, and there are hairs on the last inch of the tail.

Spotted Cat

Spotted Cats are a British short-haired breed. They are believed by some to have been the original domestic cat in that country, and appeared in the earliest cat shows. The breed died out, however, and it was not until 1960 that serious efforts (involving Silver Tabbies and Black Shorthairs) were made to recreate it. 'Spotties' were given their own standard in 1966.

The body of a show Spotted Cat should be of medium length, powerfully built, and thick set, with a full chest, and short, strong legs. The tail is rather short, and thick at the base, tapering slightly at the tip.

The head should be broad with well-developed cheeks, small slightly rounded ears, and large round eyes that compliment the coat color.

The coat is short and fine. The markings must be distinct spots that contrast well with the ground color; they may be round or oblong, but bars or even broken stripes are considered faults. The spots should cover the entire body. Tabby markings on the face and head are acceptable.

Spotted Cats can be any color in Spec-

Left: Silver Spotted Cat.

trum A (see Colors and Patterns) as long as there is good contrast between ground color and markings. Brown, Red, and Silver are the most popular colors.

Spotted Cat, Little
See Tiger Cat

Stumpy
See Manx

Sumatran Tiger
See Tiger

Supilak

The Supilak, or Copper, is a copper-colored cat from Thailand. It has been recognized as a breed in America, but is not eligible for show competition.

Swamp Cat
See Jungle Cat

Swimming Cat
See Turkish Van Cat

Right : Brown Tabby Short-hair (Classic Pattern). Below : Brown Tabby Persian (Long-hair) kitten. Note the copper eyes and classic markings. Overleaf : An adult Brown Tabby Short-hair on show.

Swiss Mountain Cat
See European Wild Cat

Tabby

The term 'Tabby' is usually applied to any cat with stripes and bars, although the standard for show cats is quite specific about the desired patterning (see Colors and Patterns). It has been claimed that if all the domestic cats in the world were to interbreed, eventually all cats would be tabbies. The 'M' on the forehead is said to be the mark of Mohammed.

The standard for markings applies to both Tabby Persians and Tabby Short-hairs. The two patterns, Classic and Mackerel, are classed together in Britain and separately in the United States. Conformation should be that of either the Persian or the appropriate short-hair (see Persian; American Short-hair; British Short-hair). The most common Tabby varieties are Brown, Red, and Silver; in America, Tabbies are also recognized in Blue, Cameo and Cream.

Brown Tabby Persian
Once very popular, Brown Tabby Persians have become difficult to breed and today few are shown. If like-to-like mating is impossible, the best results will be achieved by mating a Brown Tabby with a Black or a dark Blue and then back to a Brown Tabby. Silver Tabbies lighten the ground color and discolor the eyes; Red Tabbies tend to weaken the conformation. Brindling is becoming a common fault in Brown Tabby Persians.

Red Tabby Persian
Some people believe that this is a male only cat; however, Red to Red mating will produce both sexes.

Silver Tabby Persian
This breed is no longer popular since it is extremely difficult to perfect. Often the markings are smudged and unclear, and brown or bronze tinges tend to creep into the coloring. There is also a problem in finding a mate that will improve the conformation without damaging the markings. Kittens are born nearly all black, and the silver appears after about four months. Kittens *born* with tabby markings often prove to be badly patterned adults.

Blue Tabby Persian
This breed was officially recognized in America in 1962 and first appeared in Brown Tabby litters.

Brown Tabby Short-hair
One of the oldest known breeds, this cat's appearance as a pedigreed cat is relatively rare. It is rather difficult to find the right stud; like-to-like matings are likely to lead to deterioration of conformation.

Red Tabby Short-hair
These cats are often marmalade, ginger, or sandy cats. Red Tabby males are often mated with Tortoiseshells or Calicos (both virtually all-female varieties), though it sometimes is difficult to eliminate the tabby markings once they have been introduced.

Silver Tabby Short-hair
The Silver Tabby Short-hair is the most popular of the Tabby Short-hairs. Kittens are born with clear markings that fade and then re-establish themselves at about three months. Silver Tabby conformation is usually better than that of the other types, and Blacks are often introduced to maintain the standard.

Tabby Colorpoint Short-hair
See Colorpoint Short-hair (Lynx Point)

Tabby Point
See Colorpoint Short-hair

Temminck's Golden Cat
Felis temmincki

Temminck's Golden Cat is widely distributed throughout north India, Tibet, southwest China, and Southeast Asia. It is believed to exist in three varieties which seems reasonable considering the large area it covers.

It prefers lightly forested areas and is known to be a good climber, but little else is known of its habits; its prey is believed to include mammals up to the size of small deer and some have been shot while attempting to kill domestic stock. It is said to be easily tamed as a kitten and there are some reports of it being trained to obey and do tricks, like a dog.

An adult Temminck's Golden Cat is about 4.5 feet long (including a 1.5-foot tail) with a thick build, powerful legs, and large feet. The tail is not tapered.

The thick, soft coat is usually a deep golden red that lightens slightly on the neck, chest, and underparts. (Color can vary from location to location, however.) There are distinctive black streaks mingled with white on the face and head.

Tiger
Panthera tigris

The Tiger originated in Siberia, but with the coming of the Ice Age it was forced to move southward, adapting itself to new habitats. At its peak it could be found in a vast area from the Caspian Sea to the Manchurian coast, throughout China, India, and Southeast Asia.

Today, however, its range and numbers have been greatly reduced and the entire species is in grave danger of extinction: there were some 30,000 tigers in 1939, while today there are less than 2000.

There are several reasons for this destruction. The many wars in Asia over the last thirty years wrecked havoc on both the tigers and their habitat – especially in Vietnam, where defoliating chemicals decimated the tigers along with their habitat and food supply. The encroachment of civilization with its land reclamation projects, hydro-electric plants, and so on, has taken its toll. And exploitation for their skins, despite efforts by several governments to curb it, continues to be a major threat.

Bengal or Indian Tiger.

Two exceptionally rare tigers: on the left is the White Tiger, a dilute form of the Indian or Bengal Tiger; on the right is the very rare Sumatran Tiger.

There are eight species of Tiger:

Bali Tiger
Panthera tigris balica
This, the smallest and darkest of Tigers, is now extinct.

Bengal Tiger or *Indian Tiger*
Pt tigris
Although the most numerous species today, the Bengal Tiger is still in need of protection.

Caspian Tiger or *Persian Tiger*
Pt virgata
Very rare and verging on extinction.

Chinese Tiger
Pt amoyensis
The Chinese Tiger is in all likelihood extinct.

Indo-Chinese Tiger or *Manchurian Tiger*
Pt corbetti
This Tiger is the largest and most powerful species but its numbers are decreasing rapidly.

Javan Tiger
Pt sondiaca
This small Tiger with a dark coat is bordering on total extinction.

Siberian Tiger
Pt altaica
The Siberian Tiger is paler than the others, with a long, thick, shaggy coat.

Sumatran Tiger
Pt sumatrae
The Sumatran Tiger is also very rare.

It is sometimes possible to distinguish between these species, though individual Tigers vary so much in size and markings that it is often very difficult. In general,
northern Tigers are bigger and paler than their southern cousins.

Tigers prefer thick cover and dislike excessive heat; during the hottest part of the day they will retire to a cove or a shallow pool. Their hearing is exceptional but their sight is poor, and if a victim is camouflaged and stays very still it will often go undetected. Their diet is varied and is dictated largely by the region; it can include monkeys, deer, domestic stock, and other animals. Tigers have even been known to attack elephants.

They are very solitary animals; males and females only come together for short periods during the mating season. During this time, however, the male will be extremely possessive and will not allow another male near. The female usually has her first litter at about three years of age, and every three years after that. Usual litters are from two to four cubs, who are born complete with markings and weighing two to four pounds. They are born blind and helpless, and remain with their mother until they are about two years old.

The largest tigers can be twelve feet long from head to tail and weigh about 500 pounds; the smallest are about half that size. Tigresses are usually much smaller than the males.

Color varies from buff or pale fawn to rich brown, with dark brown stripes. The number and width of these stripes varies considerably among individuals, not regions. They run vertically on the body, from the center of the back down the sides, and horizontally on the legs. There are more stripes on the rump than on the shoulders. The tail is ringed and ends in a dark brown tip. There are no markings on the nose, but the rest of the head is evenly striped.

A dilute form called the White Tiger has occasionally appeared in India; it is almost white with light brown stripes, blue eyes, and a pink nose.

Tiger Cat
Felis tigrina

The Tiger Cat, also known as the Little Spotted Cat, is another endangered species, in part because it is extensively hunted for its skin.

It inhabits forests and woodlands from Costa Rica in Central America to northern South America. It is an excellent climber, and hunts birds and small mammals.

Tiger Cats do not make good pets – in fact, several people have died trying to tame them. They are quite fierce as kittens and become even more vicious as they grow older.

The Tiger Cat is easily confused with the Margay, though the average size is a bit smaller – perhaps three feet including tail. Markings on the Tiger Cat, moreover, are not as distinct as those on the Ocelot and Margay. A row of dark spots runs down the back, enlarging and forming rosettes on the flanks and sides. The center of the rosettes is darker than the ground color, which is fawn with a grayish tinge. The rosettes become spots again on the legs, gradually becoming smaller until they fade out entirely on the paws. The tail is ringed with large dark blotches. There are dark streaks and white bars on the cheeks and around the eyes, and the whisker pads are spotted.

Tonkinese

The Tonkinese was produced in the United States by crossing a Siamese and a Burmese. It is now being bred on both sides of the Atlantic, in Australia and New Zealand, but has not been recognized.

Tortie

The word 'Tortie' is a commonly used abbreviation for Tortoiseshell.

Tortie Point
See Colorpoint Short-hair; Himalayan

Tortoiseshell and White Long-hair and Short-hair
See Calico

Tortoiseshell Burmese
See Burmese

Tortoiseshell Cameo
See Cameo

Below: Tiger Cat.
Left: Tortoiseshell and White Short-hair.

Tortoiseshell Persian

The coat of this striking cat should be long and patterned with distinct patches of deep rich black, red, and cream. Black should not be predominant. (See also Colors and Patterns.)

Tri-colored cats are one of the oldest known varieties, but they were usually products of random matings. However, cats with tabby markings, stray white hairs, and blurred, indistinct patches, are usually unacceptable as show cats.

The Tortoiseshell Persian is very difficult to reproduce to the high standard required of show cats. It is virtually an all female breed (the few males born are al-

Right:
Tortoiseshell
Persian (or Long-
hair).
Below:
Tortoiseshell Short-
hair.

ways sterile), so like-to-like breeding is impossible. Instead, breeders must use a Black or Cream male and a Tortie female, with completely unpredictable results.

Conformation should be that of the Persian.

Tortoiseshell Short-hair

Tortoiseshell Short-hairs should conform to the short-hair standard (see American Short-hair or British Short-hair), with the markings described in Colors and Patterns. Breeding these attractive, playful cats is subject to the same difficulties and uncertainties described for the Tortoiseshell Persian.

Turkish Angora
See Angora

Turkish Van Cat

The Turkish Van Cat comes from the Lake Van area of Turkey where it has been kept as a domestic pet for centuries. It is also known as the Van Cat or Swimming Cat. This cat loves nothing more than a swim or a bath in warm (about body temperature) water although care must be taken to see that the animal is thoroughly dried after its dip to prevent colds.

Litters usually consist of only two kittens which are, more often than not, males. Kittens are born with markings that are usually more pronounced than in adults.

A few of these attractive and affectionate pets have been imported to England, where they were recognized in 1969, but they are still comparatively rare outside Turkey.

The conformation of the Turkish Van Cat is similar to the Angora. It should have a long, sturdy body on medium-length legs; a thick, muscular neck and shoulders; a blunt, medium-length tail; round paws with tufted toes; and a small wedge-shaped head. The ears are large and rounded and are set upright, quite close together. The eyes are round and the nose rather long.

The coat consists of a wooly undercoat and long, silky hairs. The color should be chalk white without any yellowish traces. There are auburn splotches on the head and auburn rings on the tail. The background color on the tail is a lighter shade of auburn. Ears are white with a slight pinkish tinge on the inside. Nose leather and paw pads are shell pink.

Van Cat
See Turkish Van Cat

White Persian

This beautiful and popular variety owes much of its development to the Angora. Thus, its conformation differs a bit from the Persian standards (see Persian): its body is slightly longer, the face not quite so round, the ears slightly larger and the nose longer.

The long, silky coat should be pure white; any yellow staining is a fault.

Whites are usually bred by mating Whites with Blacks, Blues, or Creams. Like-to-like mating is difficult and must be carefully planned.

Although they are a fastidious variety they do require frequent grooming. Grease will stain the fur, and a warm bath a few days before a show will vastly improve their appearance. There are three recognized types of White Persian, based solely on eye color.

Blue-Eyed White
This type of White Persian was the first

Left: Turkish Van Cat.
Above: White Blue-eyed Persian kitten.

to be bred. Unfortunately they are almost always deaf. Until recently, this type was rapidly declining in numbers, but breeders are now making a determined effort to re-establish it by introducing Blue Persians and the other two White varieties into their breeding programs. Cats born with a small dark smudge on the underparts usually have good hearing, and there is also the possibility that the smudge will fade as they mature making them suitable for showing. The blue eye color is difficult to reproduce; green eyes are a fault.

Odd-Eyed White
This breed appears in litters of both Blue-Eyed and Orange-Eyed Whites. They were recognized in Britain in 1968. They are not deaf, though many claim that they are hard of hearing on the side that has the blue eye. Conformation is generally better than in Blue-Eyed Whites.

Orange-Eyed White
This breed resulted from a chance mating between a Blue-Eyed White and another

Persian with orange eyes. They were recognized during the 1930s. Their breeding is much more predictable than for the Blue-Eyed; they usually have a better conformation; they are not deaf.

White Short-hair

Conformation should be that of the short-hair standard (see American Short-hair; British Short-hair). The coat should be fine and soft, pure white with no trace of colored hairs and no tinge of yellow. Like the White Persian, the White Short-hair is recognized in three varieties based on eye color.

Blue-Eyed White
This popular, but rather rare cat is hard to breed with outstanding conformation. Most Blue-Eyed Whites are deaf; those with a dark smudge on their heads between the ears usually have good hearing.

Odd-Eyed White
This breed with one blue eye and one orange, is not deaf, and plays a useful role in breeding both other varieties. They can be found in both Blue-Eyed and Orange-Eyed litters.

Orange-Eyed White
Like the other White Short-hairs, Orange-Eyed Whites are born with blue eyes which then, however, turn slowly to orange as the cat matures. The orange deepens with age and often turns to a coppery color in adulthood. This variety has good hearing.

White Tiger
See Tiger

Wild Cat, African
See African Wild Cat

Wild Cat, European
See European Wild Cat

Wild Cat, Scottish
See European Wild Cat

Zibeline
See Burmese

Right : Lynx with her kitten. The kitten was partially tamed by the photographer before this picture was taken.

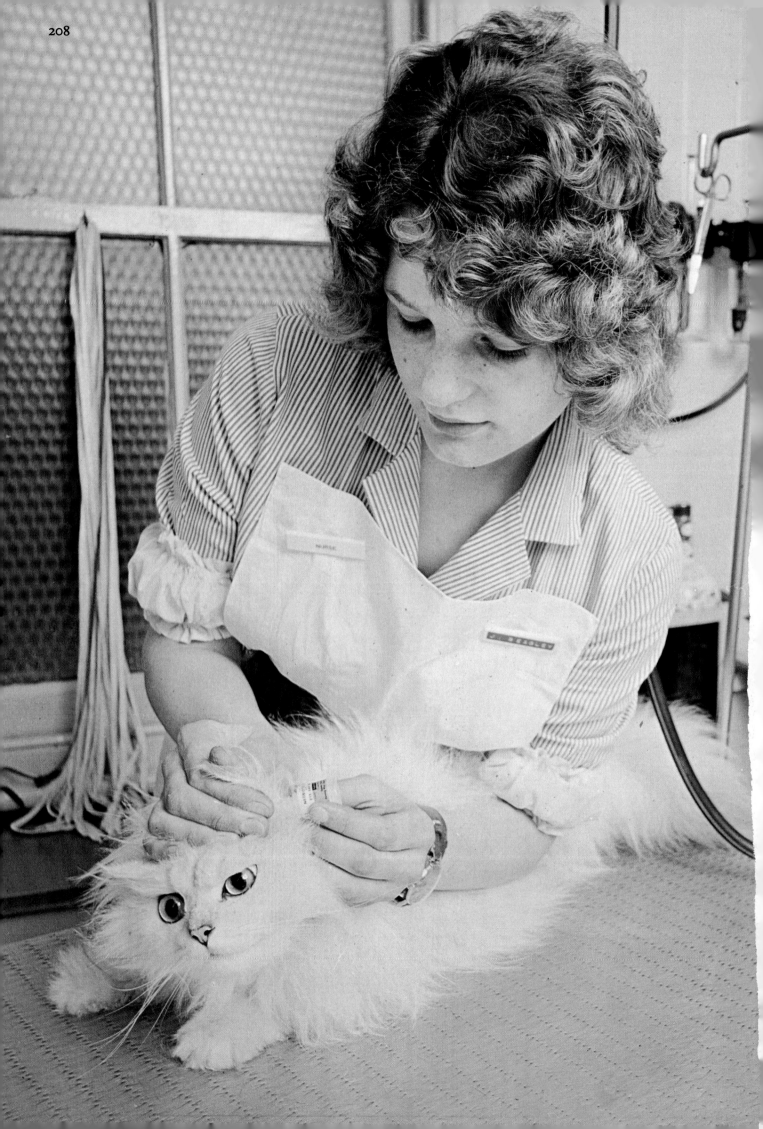